PEARSON CUSTOM LIBRARY

ENGLISH
MERCURY READER

Dr. Veronica Thompson
Athabasca University

PEARSON

Senior Vice President, Editorial: Patrick F. Boles
Senior Sponsoring Editor: Natalie Danner
Development Editor: Jill Johnson
Operations Manager: Eric M. Kenney
Production Manager: Jennifer Berry
Rights Manager: Michael E. Mushlitz
Art Director: Renée Sartell
Cover Designers: Kristen Kiley, Blythe Russo, Tess Mattern, and Renée Sartell

Cover Art: "Gigantia Mountains & Sea of Cortes," by R.G.K. Photography, Copyright © Tony Stone Images; "Dime," courtesy of the Shaw Collection; "Open Book On Table Edge w/Pencil," courtesy of PhotoAlto Photography/Veer Incorporated; "Open Book On Table Near Table's Corner," courtesy of Fancy Photography/Veer Incorporated; "Scrabble Pieces and a Die," by G. Herbst, courtesy of PlainPicture Photography/Veer Incorporated; "Binary codes in bowls," by John Still, courtesy of Photographer's Choice/Getty Images; "Close-up of an open book," courtesy of Glowimages/Getty Images; "College Students Sitting At Tables," courtesy of Blend/PunchStock; "Red and blue circles," courtesy of Corbis Images; "Laptop screen showing photograph of landscape," courtesy of Martin Holtcamp/Getty Images; "Apples flying," courtesy of Arne Morgenstern/Getty Images; "Riverdance," by Angela Sciaraffa; "Stone path leading through a garden" and "Book pages" courtesy of Getty Images, Inc; "Chicago" by Kristen Kiley.

Printed in Canada

Please visit our website at *www.pearsonlearningsolutions.com*.

Attention bookstores: For permission to return any unsold stock, contact us at *pe-uscustomreturns@pearson.com*.

Pearson Learning Solutions, 501 Boylston Street, Suite 900, Boston, MA 02116
A Pearson Education Company
www.pearsoned.com

PEARSON   ISBN 10: 0-536-89745-X
ISBN 13: 978-0-536-89745-9

General Editors

Janice Neuleib
Illinois State University

Kathleen Shine Cain
Merrimack College

Stephen Ruffus
Salt Lake Community College

Table of Contents

Argument: Non-Traditional Model

Argument and Persuasion

A hundred and fifty years ago, many prominent Americans were engaged in a heated debate over slavery. Abolitionists (opponents of slavery) cited the Declaration of Independence, claiming that "all men are created equal" and decrying an institution that allowed one person to be the property of another. Slaveholders pointed to the Bible, claiming that the Old Testament identified certain races as "sons of Cain," destined to be enslaved throughout history. Eventually the slavery issue was settled by the Civil War, but prior to and during that conflict, speakers and writers engaged in **argument** about the legitimacy of slavery. Put simply, argument refers to the presentation of a claim (e.g., that slavery should be abolished) and evidence (e.g., citations from the Declaration, stories of mistreated slaves) to support it. Those engaged in argument seek to persuade their audience to accept a certain position or take a certain action. While argument and persuasion are not precisely synonymous, their purposes are similar. **Persuasion** seeks to sway an audience, often employing appeals to emotion; **argument** seeks to justify a position, always employing appeals to reason and sometimes appeals to emotion as well. As in the case of the abolition debate, the most effective arguments involve appeals to both reason and emotion. In this chapter, we will discuss three models of argument: **Rogerian**, based on the work of psychologist Carl Rogers; **Toulmin**, based on the work of philosopher Stephen Toulmin; and **Aristotelian** or **classical**, based on the work of the great philosopher Aristotle.

Although slavery has not been an issue for over a century, race remains one of the most debated issues in contemporary society. Most of the examples in this chapter will be drawn from this issue.

1

In examining arguments about race, we will refer to a chapter from Maya Angelou's memoir *I Know Why the Caged Bird Sings*. Titled "Graduation," it recounts the day in 1940 on which Angelou graduated from the Lafayette County Training School, a segregated school in Arkansas. This piece (included at the end of this chapter) serves as an effective example of argument that is not presented in traditional argument form. Written as a narrative, "Graduation" nonetheless argues vehemently against the racism that supported legal segregation in schools during the first half of this century. It still resonates today, despite the demise of legal segregation, because issues of affirmative action and racial equality continue to be part of our national debates.

Evidence

Both argument and persuasion share one crucial quality: Their claims must be supported by evidence. That evidence may take the form of reasoning, appeals to authority, reference to statistics or facts, or appeals to the audience's needs or values. Regardless of the nature of the supporting evidence, that support must be presented for an argument to be legitimate. This is what differentiates argument from mere **statement of opinion**. In contemporary society, statement of opinion is often mistaken for argument. If you listen to talk-radio programs or tabloid television, you hear endless unsubstantiated opinions presented as if they were full-blown arguments. Such programs do little except reinforce existing beliefs shared by the audience precisely because no argument is taking place. The key to convincing an audience of the legitimacy of a claim lies not in stating the claim but in supporting it with evidence. This chapter will explore the various kinds of support used to justify claims made in arguments.

Inductive and Deductive Reasoning

In constructing arguments based on rational rather than emotional appeals, it is necessary to understand the distinction between the two primary types of reasoning. **Inductive reasoning** involves moving from specific evidence to a general conclusion, while **deductive reasoning** moves from a general statement to specific conclusions. Using inductive reasoning to persuade her audience of the lack of equity in segregated schools, for example, Angelou bases her argument on a collection of specific pieces of evidence:

Evidence: Segregated schools are poorly funded.

Segregated schools have outdated facilities.

Segregated schools train students for menial jobs.

Conclusion: Segregated schools are inherently unequal to white schools.

A deductive approach, on the other hand, involves presenting a **syllogism**. A syllogism comprises three parts: the **major premise** (a general statement about a category or class), the **minor premise** (a specific statement about one member of that category or class), and the **conclusion** (derived about the specific member). If presented in the form of a syllogism, Maya Angelou's argument against segregation might look like this:

Major premise: Segregation is always unjust.

Minor premise: The school system of Stamps, Arkansas was segregated in the 1940s.

Conclusion: The school system of Stamps, Arkansas in the 1940s was unjust.

Looking at Angelou's piece in this way illustrates the interrelationship between rational arguments and emotional appeals. While the syllogism is valid, the real persuasive power of "Graduation" lies in the emotional response it engenders in readers. Similarly, the emotional appeal would lose its effectiveness if the rational argument were not valid.

As you are probably aware from looking at this syllogism, it is necessary for the major premise to be valid in all cases if the conclusion is to be viable. For example, if it were demonstrated that segregation was not always unjust, then the conclusion would no longer follow. The conclusion would then have to be amended.

Audience

All models of argument emphasize **audience**. Because the most basic goal of argument is to convince the audience of the legitimacy of a claim, the arguer must be aware of the knowledge, values, and needs of the audience. In seeking to convince her readers to fight racism, for example, Angelou must consider a variety of audiences. Some will be entirely sympathetic to her position, some antithetic, and many will fall somewhere between those two extremes. Her task in making an argument is to appeal to common **beliefs** and **values** of her audience. By focusing on the aspirations of the children of Stamps, Angelou seeks to appeal to beliefs and values shared by everyone in her audience, namely that children represent the hope of a culture. This appeal makes her argument more convincing even to those who might believe in segregation.

Acknowledging/Rebutting Opposition

Acknowledgment of opposing arguments is an essential component of any audience-based model of argument. Acknowledging the opposition enhances the arguer's credibility and strengthens the argument as well. Regardless of the nature of the rebuttal, it is essential to the strength and validity of the argument that opposing views be aired and dealt with.

Of course, on some issues the credibility of one position has been so eroded that there is little if any validity left in it. Legal segregation, for example, has been judged an entirely untenable practice since the civil rights movement of the 1960s. Thus Maya Angelou does not need to acknowledge opposing views in order to establish her credibility; her piece (indeed, the entire book in which it appears) highlights past injustices in order to eradicate any remnants of unjust practices that remain, as well as to prevent such injustices from recurring in the future.

Current arguments in favor of retaining racial considerations in public college and university admissions, however, do need to acknowledge the opposition. Opponents of such admissions policies frequently refer to Martin Luther King's call for judging people by the content of their character rather than the color of their skin. If you are arguing to retain racial considerations, you must acknowledge that color does play a role in such admissions programs. In rebutting the "color-blind" argument, you might point to unequal educational opportunities for many minority students in elementary and high schools. This inequity, you might argue, requires redress when these students apply to college.

The Rogerian Model of Argument

In preparing an argument it is important to consider various approaches to argument and persuasion. Two of the more common approaches used today are the **Rogerian** and the **Toulmin** models. While this chapter focuses primarily on the Toulmin model, the Rogerian model is worth studying for its emphasis on common ground. This model was developed from psychologist Carl Rogers's work on conflict. Noting that adversarial arguments often result in opponents becoming entrenched in their own positions, Rogers suggested an approach that seeks common ground in order to negotiate a mutually acceptable position. Using the Rogerian model, you would first acknowledge your opposition and assert its validity, and then find a common ground from which all sides can view the issue. Finally, you would present evidence to establish your position as the most reasonable. Arguments for and against racial considerations in college admissions provide an example of the Rogerian model. An outline of the argument might look something like this:

A. **Acknowledge opposing position** that racial considerations in public college and university admissions do not result in each student's being judged solely on merit (i.e., some minority students may be admitted over equally qualified non-minority students).

B. **Find common ground**, namely that both sides are interested in eliminating racial inequities.

C. **Present evidence** that the benefits of racial considerations in public college and university admissions outweigh the costs (i.e., racial considerations at this level address inequities in elementary and secondary education).

Arguers who use the Rogerian approach truly seek to persuade their audience rather than to win an argument. However, not all persuasive pieces lend themselves to the Rogerian approach. When the opposition is generally discredited, it is difficult to acknowledge its validity. Thus in an argument such as Angelou's against segregation, the Rogerian model would not be appropriate. For Angelou's purposes, the Toulmin model is more appropriate.

The Toulmin Model of Argument

In 1958, philosopher Stephen Toulmin published *The Uses of Argument*, a book that challenged traditional logic-based argument models. Toulmin based his model on the adversarial process of a courtroom, in which each position is challenged openly and judged by a third party. Toulmin's model emphasizes the audience of an argument, and charges the arguer with not only providing support for his or her position, but with acknowledging and rebutting the opposition as well. The key to the Toulmin model is a strong link between the thesis and the evidence supporting that thesis. The primary components of the Toulmin model are **claim** (thesis), **grounds** (evidence or emotional appeal), and **warrant** (assumption linking claim to grounds).

Claims

If you are arguing for retaining racial consideration in public college and university admissions, you may seek to persuade your audience in several ways. In addressing those who argue for purely merit-based admissions, you may simply want to establish that this position is valid and must be considered in any debate. You also may want to convince those who call racial considerations a form of racism that you simply seek to level the playing field for students who have been denied opportunities in elementary and secondary school. Or you may seek to convince those who agree with you to take such actions as picketing institutions that have eliminated racial considerations, engaging in letter-writing campaigns to major newspapers, or petitioning legislators to retain racial considerations.

The purpose of an argument is embedded in the claim, the point that the arguer wants to make. The thesis of an argument, whether stated or implied, presents the claim. Claims can be divided into three primary categories: claims of fact, claims of value, and claims of policy. The type of claim depends on the purpose of the argument; in turn, the structure and development of the argument depends largely on the type of claim being presented.

Claims of fact are assertions about the existence of a certain condition. In an argument about racial considerations, proponents and opponents alike may wish to establish certain facts about such policies in order to frame their arguments. Competing claims of fact regarding this issue include the following:

Claim 1: Racial considerations offer preferential treatment to some students based on color rather than on merit exclusively.

Claim 2: Educational inequities at the elementary and secondary levels reduce opportunities for many African-American students.

In each case, the claim must be supported by data, hard evidence that establishes the existence of the condition stated in the claim.

Claims of value are statements of judgment regarding the worth of something. While Maya Angelou does present claims of fact in "Graduation" (e.g., that facilities in black schools were inferior to those in white schools), she also addresses issues of values. A claim of value made in Angelou's "Graduation" might read,

Claim: Segregating black children in schools is morally repugnant.

Often based on tastes or moral beliefs, claims of value must be supported by establishing criteria by which the judgments are made.

Claims of policy are calls to action. One of Maya Angelou's goals in writing "Graduation" was to eliminate school segregation. The following claim of policy reflects that goal:

Claim: Segregation in public schools must be eliminated.

Claims of policy must be supported by reasons for taking a specific action. Reasons for eliminating segregation, according to Angelou, include the equality of black and white children and the rights of all children to pursue their dreams.

In order for a claim to be effective, the terms of the claim must be clearly defined. For example, the above claim refers to public schools only, meaning that the argument is aimed at schools funded by state and local governments, not by private organizations.

Grounds

Grounds, also called *support* or *supporting evidence*, comprise everything the arguer offers to justify a claim. Grounds may include **facts, data, statistics, opinions of experts or affected individuals, examples**, and **appeals to emotion**. The nature of the grounds normally depends upon the type of claim being presented.

Facts offered in support of a claim should be irrefutable. That the black Lafayette County Training School has a dirt playground and no sports equipment while the white Central School has a paved playground and a variety of equipment is a fact that Maya Angelou can point to in her implicit argument against segregated schools.

Data and *statistics* offer numerical evidence to support a claim. Arguers must be careful, however, to recognize that statistics can be interpreted in different ways. Recently, for example, a good deal of attention has been paid to the depression and suicide statistics of homosexual teenagers. Those arguing for homosexual rights point to the statistics as evidence of the effects of ostracism on young gays and lesbians, while those arguing that homosexuality is abnormal use the same statistics to demonstrate the troubled state of mind and the guilt of homosexual teenagers. If you wish to make a convincing argument for retaining racial considerations in public college and university admissions, you must be careful to offer statistics that are less open to interpretation. Or you can offer the opinion of recognized experts.

The *opinion of experts* is valuable not only to support a particular interpretation of statistics but also to lend credibility to a claim. The opinion of someone whose expertise in a community is acknowledged is far more valuable than that of an uninformed person. In arguing for racial considerations, for example, the opinion of a respected educator or sociologist would offer strong support for the claim.

The *opinion of affected individuals* is also effective. In "Graduation," Angelou writes of her reaction to a speech by Edward Donleavy, a white politician who reminds his audience of their second-class status:

> The man's dead words fell like bricks around the auditorium and too many settled in my belly. . . . It was awful to be a Negro and have no control over my life. It was brutal to be young and already trained to sit quietly and listen to charges brought against my color with no chance of defense. We should all be dead.

These descriptions of the author's state of mind after being belittled by Donleavy offer convincing support for her position on the human impact of segregation.

Examples provide support for claims if they can be used in such a way that the audience draws generalizations from them. Angelou's example of a segregated school, if readers consider it representative, will support her claim.

Appeals to emotion differ from other grounds in that they do not rely on logic. Instead, appeals to emotion attempt to forge a link between the arguer and the audience by focusing on the needs of the audience or the values shared with the audience. Appealing to the values of her audience, Maya Angelou focuses on the industriousness and aspirations of the children in Stamps. She is proud of her own academic record:

> No absences, no tardiness, and my academic work was among the best of the year. . . . I could say the preamble to the Constitution even faster than Bailey. . . . I had memorized the presidents of the United States from Washington to Roosevelt in chronological as well as alphabetical order.

And she implies that both she and her classmates aspired to be more than "carpenters, farmers, handymen, masons, maids, cooks and baby nurses"; indeed, her brother Bailey wants to become a lawyer, even though it means that he must "first pay penance for his skin by picking cotton and hoeing corn and studying correspondence books at night for twenty years." Americans are known to value industriousness and aspirations; therefore, by emphasizing both qualities in her piece, Angelou uses her audience's own values to support her position.

Warrants

Perhaps the least familiar of the three components of the Toulmin model, the **warrant** is nonetheless crucial to the success of an argument. Put simply, the warrant is the assumption or belief, shared by the arguer and the audience, that underlies the entire argument. A warrant can be considered a guarantee for the argument, or, as Toulmin himself referred to it, a bridge between the claim and the grounds. Maya Angelou's argument, including the warrant, might look like this:

> **Claim:** Segregation is wrong.
>
> **Grounds:** Segregation results in poorer facilities for black students; segregation denies qualified black students higher education; segregation dehumanizes black people.
>
> **Warrant:** Any system advocating inequality or dehumanization is wrong.

If the audience shares Angelou's assumptions about equality and humanity, then her claim and grounds will be convincing.

Backing

Warrants such as those just illustrated are *implicit*; that is, they are obvious to any reasonable person. Occasionally, however, it is necessary to make the warrant *explicit*. Consider, for example, the 1954 Supreme Court decision in *Brown v. Board of Education of Topeka, Kansas*. The claim represented in that decision is similar to Angelou's: Segregation is unconstitutional. The grounds are also similar: Segregation results in poorer facilities for black students. In 1954, however, it was necessary that the warrant be spelled out: Separate facilities are inherently unequal. At the time, such an assumption was not common; thus the Court had to make the warrant clear. Whether the warrant is explicit or implicit, if it effectively links the grounds to the claim, then the argument will itself be effective.

If the warrant is not explicit, that is if it is not necessarily shared by the audience, then it must be supported by **backing**. Just as the grounds support the claim, the backing supports the warrant. As with other evidence, backing can take several different forms. Chief Justice Earl Warren, for example, in offering backing for the warrant on which the *Brown* decision was based, cited the fact that during the time of the 1896 *Plessy v. Ferguson* decision, in which the Court ruled that separate facilities were not inherently unequal, public education did not serve the purpose it did in 1954. Calling late nineteenth-century education "rudimentary," Warren noted that rural schools often combined several grades, that often the school year was a mere three months long, and that compulsory attendance was not enforced. In 1954, on the other hand, education was "the very foundation of good citizenship" as well as a necessary component to success in the workplace. Warren also cited the opinion of experts in his warrant, noting that psychologists in the 1950s agreed that segregation implied inferiority and therefore impeded black children's motivation. This backing for the Court's argument was necessary precisely because assumptions about the role of education and the effects of segregation had changed substantially between 1896 and 1954.

Qualifiers

Another significant term used in the Toulmin model is the **qualifier**. Consider the absolute nature of the following claim: *All* public college and university admissions policies based on racial considerations address previous educational inequities. To render this claim invalid, a single example of an upper-middle-class minority student who has benefited from such a policy would suffice. A strategy that you might use then is to attach a qualifier to the claim:

> **Qualified claim:** In most cases, public college and university admissions policies based on racial considerations address previous educational inequities.

Amending claims to include qualifiers can facilitate an argument by heading off opposing claims before they can be made.

The Aristotelian Model of Argument

The earliest analyses of argument in Western thought can be found in the writings of the ancient Greeks, particularly Aristotle. Aristotle's *Rhetoric* identifies three means by which an arguer attempts to persuade an audience: **logos**, or rational appeals; **ethos**, or emphasis on the integrity of the arguer; and **pathos**, or emotional appeals. As these terms indicate, traditional Aristotelian argument focuses not only on appeals to reason but to emotion and to integrity or credibility as well.

Logos

Considered the most important category of proof by rhetoricians from Aristotle to the present, *logos* appeals to the rational mind. *Logos* refers to the internal consistency of the argument, as well as to its reliance on reason and common sense. The *logos* of an argument favoring racial considerations in public college and university admissions policies is illustrated by the testimony of experts regarding the impact of such policies, as well as statistics suggesting inequities in elementary and secondary education.

Categories of Logical Proof

Logical proof in an argument can be presented in a number of ways. The nature of the claim, the type of grounds, and the nature of the warrant all determine the type of proof or line of reasoning employed to support the warrant. We will discuss six specific lines of reasoning: **argument from generalization**, **argument from definition**, **argument from cause**, **argument from sign**, **argument from analogy**, and **argument from parallel case**.

Argument from generalization is also known as *inductive reasoning*. Generalization involves offering a series of examples that when taken together support a position. For example, when Angelou points to a class full of bright, ambitious students whose aspirations are denied because of segregation, it is reasonable to conclude that segregation is unjust. The resulting argument would look like this:

Argument: Segregation denies the aspirations of bright, ambitious students.

Support: All of the bright, ambitious students at the Lafayette County Training School were denied opportunities because of segregation.

Argument from definition calls upon the arguer to establish a common understanding of key terms with the audience. If such an understanding does not exist, then the argument cannot proceed. Chief Justice Earl Warren, in his decision in *Brown v. Board of Education*, found it necessary to define public education in order to make his case. Claiming that public education in the 1950s was designed to prepare students for citizenship, he then made the case that separate facilities placed unconstitutional burdens on blacks relegated to those facilities. Taken as an argument itself, Warren's definition can be outlined as follows:

Argument: Segregated schools are by definition unequal.

Support: Segregated schools do not offer black children the opportunity to learn good citizenship, one of the functions of public education.

Argument from cause posits that a specific action results in a specific effect. In presenting a causation argument, it is necessary to link the cause to the effect; the audience must be convinced that the situation presented is not coincidence. Maya Angelou, in arguing that limited opportunities for black children was an effect of segregation in schools, establishes the relationship between inferior schools and limited opportunity. Her argument from cause would look like this:

Argument: Segregated schools limited the career opportunities of black children.

Support: Black schools had few facilities and fewer programs to prepare students for a variety of careers.

Argument from sign focuses on symptoms or indicators of a particular condition. Some of the most obvious signs with which we are familiar are symptoms of disease: stuffy nose, a cough, and a fever are signs of a cold. Although there is not always a causal relationship between the sign and the condition indicated, argument from sign can nevertheless be effective. You might argue, for example, that racially intolerant attitudes are a sign of a campus that is homogeneous, or lacking in diversity. The lack of diversity may not have caused the intolerant attitudes; nonetheless, the attitudes signify a homogeneous campus community. The argument from sign would look like this:

Argument: Racially intolerant attitudes are a sign of a homogeneous campus.

Support: On campuses lacking in diversity, racially intolerant attitudes are prevalent.

Argument from analogy uses an object or situation to represent an unrelated object or situation. The power of the analogy normally rests in the imagery it suggests, but at times rational connections between the two things strengthen the analogy. In taped conversations about the Watergate cover-up, White House Counsel John Dean referred to the growing scandal as a cancer eating at the presidency. Such an analogy is powerful in its imagery, but there is little real resemblance between a cancer-ridden body and the office of the presidency. An argument from analogy that calls on more rational connections would read as follows:

Argument: Like a field planted year after year with only one crop, a homogeneous campus community yields little growth.

Support: Lack of diversity makes the campus atmosphere less productive, just as overplanting a single crop year after year makes the soil less productive.

Argument from parallel case is used regularly in courts of law. Whenever an attorney cites a precedent, she is arguing from parallel case. Based on comparisons between objects or conditions with shared characteristics, argument from parallel case asks the audience to believe that what has happened in one situation can be expected to happen in another. A faulty argument from parallel case was made by the defendants in *Brown v. Board of Education*. The defense cited the 1896 *Plessy v. Ferguson* case in which separate facilities were not deemed inherently unequal. As noted previously, however, Chief Justice Warren and a majority of the Court rejected that argument, citing changing circumstances. In this case, the defense position, that conditions in 1954 replicated those in 1896, was declared faulty. A valid argument from parallel case might read as follows:

Argument:	Segregated public schools in Little Rock, Arkansas in 1960 were inherently unequal.
Support:	The Supreme Court ruled in 1954 that segregated public schools in Topeka, Kansas were inherently unequal.

Avoiding Logical Fallacies

As the example from *Brown v. Board of Education* indicates, not all arguments, even if the arguments follow a specific model, are valid. In addition to falling prey to such errors as failing to acknowledge changing times, arguers can also fall into what are known as **logical fallacies**. Such fallacies occur when the arguer is not careful in matching the grounds to the claim, or when the warrant is either irrelevant to the claim and support or is based on insubstantial backing. Logical fallacies include the following:

Post hoc reasoning assumes that simply because a phenomenon or an event precedes another, the first is the cause of the second. If a white student is denied admission to a public university which uses racial considerations in admissions decisions, the admissions policy is not necessarily the cause for denial. Any number of other causes, from the student's test scores to her intended major program of study, might have contributed to the decision.

Non sequitur (Latin for "it does not follow") is illustrated by Edward Donleavy in "Graduation" when he assumes that because he considers black students to be less than human, they will not be demoralized by his remarks. He does not take into account the limitations of his own experience, the pride of the graduates, or the heritage of the black population of Stamps.

Either/or assumes the possibility of only two diametrically opposed outcomes. To argue that colleges either maintain high admissions standards or foster racial diversity is to ignore other possibilities, for example that considering a number of criteria, including both academic standards and race, might result in a diverse institution with high standards.

Hasty generalization is also called jumping to conclusions. Just because integration of Central High School in Little Rock, Arkansas resulted in federal intervention, there was no reason to assume that all integration programs would require National Guard troops. Some communities were better prepared to abide by the *Brown v. Board of Education* decision than others.

Begging the question involves assuming that a conclusion is valid and using that conclusion as part of the argument. Donleavy in "Graduation" begs the question implicitly when he assumes that all black students aspire to be sports figures. Assuming that his conclusion is valid, he cannot see that there is no evidence to support it.

Ad hominem (Latin for "to the man") is an attack made on a person's character rather than on the position the person has taken. To discredit an opponent of affirmative action because she is in the midst of a messy divorce is to avoid the issue at hand.

Appeal to faulty authority involves attributing expertise on an issue to someone whose expertise lies in a different area. Supporting affirmative action because a leading show-business celebrity does is an example of this fallacy.

Red herring is a term for intentional diversion of attention away from an issue. Many segregationist leaders in Arkansas in the early 1960s committed this fallacy by calling up the specter of communism when confronted with civil rights activists demanding integrated schools.

False analogy ignores the fact that two analogous things or situations are not alike in all respects. Many historians now consider the analogy of the melting pot to be essentially false. While the many nationalities that make up this country, like the ingredients in a melting pot do, exist in harmony, they do not blend to become indistinguishable from one another.

It is obvious that maintaining the integrity of a logical argument is often a challenge. The legitimacy of the argument depends upon a sound relationship among the claim, the grounds, and the warrant.

Ethos

Ethos is often equal in importance to logos in an argument because it establishes the credibility and sincerity of the author. *Ethos* establishes a relationship between the arguer and the audience that supports the rational appeal of the argument. Any argument is enhanced if its author is deemed to have integrity, expertise, and a fair-minded approach. For example, Maya Angelou's *ethos* is established both within and without "Graduation." Within the essay she establishes her credibility by clearly presenting herself as one who has suffered the inequities of segregation; she has first-hand experience of her subject. A brief look at Angelou's biography also establishes her *ethos:* Growing up in the segregated South and San Francisco, she overcame numerous obstacles to become the first black female conductor on the San Francisco cable cars, to excel as an accomplished writer and actor, and to be chosen to compose and present the ceremonial poem at President Bill Clinton's first inauguration. Her experience creates sympathy in her audience, and her credentials lend credibility to her position. The establishment of credentials refers to a form of ethical proof called **argument from authority.**

Argument from authority is used to support the logical argument by calling upon the opinions of experts in the field. Because it is possible to find experts to support any number of positions in a given argument, establishing the credibility of the expert is essential. As discussed in the section on grounds, the expert should possess appropriate credentials and be respected in the field. Of course it is also essential that the authority's expertise be relevant to the topic at hand. Arguments against public school segregation after 1954 exemplify argument from authority:

Argument: Segregated schools are inherently unequal.

Support: The United States Supreme Court decided this point in 1954.

For an argument to have sound ethical appeal, it is necessary for the arguer to establish his or her own integrity, as well as the integrity of authorities cited in support of the claim.

Pathos

Pathos is perhaps the most familiar type of proof found in everyday arguments. Appealing strictly to the emotions of the audience, *pathos* can strengthen an otherwise sound rational argument by engaging the audience on a more personal level. A purely emotional argument is rarely convincing; however, expanding the appeal of an argument beyond *logos* and *ethos* can enhance it. Emotional appeals, if legitimately related to the claim, will strengthen a purely rational argument. The reason for this is simple: Human beings make decisions based on emotion as well as on reason. Indeed, sometimes emotional concerns outweigh reasonable concerns. Maya Angelou uses emotional appeals effectively in "Graduation" when she describes how she felt after Edward Donleavy's speech:

> Graduation, the hush-hush magic time of frills and gifts and congratulations and diplomas, was finished for me before my name was called. The accomplishment was nothing. The meticulous maps, drawn in three colors of ink, learning and spelling decasyllabic words, memorizing the whole of *The Rape of Lucrece*—it was for nothing. Donleavy had exposed us.

The demoralization of a young girl whose hopes only recently had included heading "for the freedom of open fields" supports the implicit argument against segregation that permeates Angelou's piece. By allowing her audience to focus not on statistics and principles but rather on a real girl's disillusionment with her life and her race, she brings the issue into clearer focus for her readers by providing a personal touch.

Language and Pathos

"Graduation" also illustrates the significance of language in *pathos*. When considering the meaning of words, it is important to distinguish between *denotation*, the dictionary definition of the word, and *connotation*, the implied meaning or emotional overtones of the word. The word *group*, for example, is rather neutral in both denotation and connotation; it refers to a number of people with some common purpose. Change the word to *gang*, however, and while the dictionary meaning may remain essentially the same, the sinister implications of the word, the sense of danger or violence, cannot be ignored. Thus a newspaper account referring to a *group* of civil rights activists creates a different image than one referring to a *gang* of activists. Angelou uses connotation when she asks why her brother has to "pay penance for his skin" in order to become a lawyer. Her reference to penance calls up religious images of sinning against God, thereby heightening the impact of this condemnation of segregation. Similarly, when she describes the demeanor of the principal and the teachers during Donleavy's speech, she writes, "the ancient tragedy was being replayed." Tragedy is often considered the highest form of drama; ancient tragedy, particularly Greek tragedy, is considered the model for everything that has followed. The implication Angelou makes, then, is that this is much more than simply an uncomfortable moment for these school officials; the scene has universal implications.

Emotional Proof
Arguments from emotion fall into two categories: **motivational appeals** and **appeals to values**. Each appeal can strengthen a rational argument.

Motivational appeals rely on an understanding of people's needs and desires. In addition to basic biological needs such as food and shelter, people also have needs for safety, for belonging, for self-expression, and so on. In "Graduation," Maya Angelou appeals to her readers' need to be perceived as good, to be approved of. When Angelou presents her arguments on the effects of segregated schools on black children, she taps into her readers' need to think themselves good, moral people. Her appeal might be presented as follows:

Argument: You should share my condemnation of segregation.

Appeal: Moral people condemn segregation, and you want to be considered a moral person.

Appeals to values rely on commonly held beliefs about what is good or desirable. (Appeals to values are similar to claims of value in the Toulmin model.) Political campaigns throughout the past two decades have focused on terms such as "family values," which, while vague and often ill-defined, nonetheless resonate with many voters. By calling upon a value shared by the audience, an arguer can strengthen a rational argument. Angelou, for example, is aware of the values of her primary audience, American readers, when she focuses on the career aspirations and the industriousness of her classmates. If her readers agree that these qualities are consistent with American values, then it is difficult for them to reject Angelou's position on segregated schools. Her argument can be outlined as follows:

Argument: Segregated schools were bad for black Americans.

Appeal: Segregated schools interfered with students' aspirations and industriousness, qualities that are valued in American society.

These lines of argument can be employed in any number of combinations. Most successful arguments will balance *logos*, *ethos*, and *pathos* in such a way that audiences are convinced not only by reason, but by authority and emotion as well.

READING AND WRITING ARGUMENTS

Now that you understand the nature of argument, you can employ that understanding in analyzing written arguments and in composing your own arguments. Using the previous discussion of the components of an effective argument to focus on specifics, you should be able to use the following advice to read argumentative texts with a critical eye.

Reading Arguments Critically

A critical reader creates a dialogue with a text by considering the author's ideas, making observations, asking questions, analyzing the author's perspective in relation to those of others, forging connections between different selections—in short, the critical reader *responds* to what the writer is saying. Responding effectively to an argument normally involves three activities: **understanding the topic**, **evaluating the evidence**, and **considering alternative perspectives**.

Understanding the Topic

A well-written argument will provide you with enough information to understand the topic at hand. But the writer is obviously presenting the material from his or her own perspective. Therefore, in order to effectively read and understand another's argument, you must first take stock of your own knowledge of the topic. This activity involves considering what you already know about the topic, clarifying your perspective on the topic, and recalling what else you may have read about the topic. If you discover that your knowledge is quite limited, you may want to investigate the topic further by talking to other students or professors and by reading about the topic in newspapers or magazines. When you begin reading the argument itself, try to identify background information presented within it. Maya Angelou, for example, describes the playground at the Lafayette County Training School and explains that the facilities at the white Central High School are far superior. Regardless of her judgment on the unfairness of these inequities, Angelou has provided readers with a sense of the conditions under which black and white children attended school prior to the *Brown v. Board of Education* decision.

More traditionally argumentative pieces include information on the topic early in the essay, often in the first paragraph.

Understanding the topic also includes identifying the claim, the grounds, and the warrant of the argument. Not all arguments are presented according to the Toulmin model, but it is possible to apply the model to most arguments. Thus the first thing to do after establishing your understanding of the piece is to highlight the author's statement of the claim. While many arguments feature clear statements of claim, some do not. Chief Justice Earl Warren, for example, states the claim clearly in his majority opinion in *Brown*: "Separate educational facilities are inherently unequal." Maya Angelou, on the other hand, never states her claim explicitly. In this case, you should state her implied claim in your own words. Those words might echo Warren's, or they might be more emotional: "Racism, as illustrated in segregated schools, demoralizes worthy black children" is one possibility.

Recognizing the grounds, or support for the claim, is the next step in reading an argument critically. The previous discussion of supporting evidence identifies several kinds of support found in Angelou's "Graduation": her identification of the industriousness and aspirations of black children, her description of the unequal facilities, and her account of the emotional toll of Donleavy's speech. Chief Justice Warren cites the changing nature of public education between 1896 and 1954, decisions in recent cases involving segregated educational facilities, and the opinions of psychologists on the effects of inferior education.

Identifying the warrant is usually a more difficult task that involves interpretation. Among Angelou's warrants are assumptions that all children should be provided with equal educational opportunities, that industriousness and aspirations are valuable American qualities, and that segregation is morally wrong. None of these warrants is stated explicitly, but a reader familiar with the Toulmin model of argument should be able to infer them from reading Angelou's narrative.

In order to facilitate your dialogue with the text, it is important to do more than simply read and identify elements passively. Underline or highlight claims and grounds; summarize them in the margins of the text; make note of questions you have regarding your understanding of certain items. If the selection includes terms that you do not understand, look them up. Often understanding one key term can turn an incomprehensible paragraph into a model of clear prose.

Evaluating the Evidence

As readers, we often take one of two contradictory approaches to a text. The first approach assumes that if the piece is published, then it must be right, so we will not question it. The second, usually occurring when we read something expressing a position contrary to our own, is simply to dismiss the argument without considering its merits. Neither approach is conducive to critical reading. In the first case, while publication lends a certain credibility to an argument, it is possible to find published arguments featuring opposing views on almost any topic. In the second case, it is necessary to understand that most published arguments are presented in the hope of continuing a dialogue on the issue. Thus to dismiss the argument out of hand is to cut off conversation. The critical reader should neither assume that the author has all the answers nor that the author has none. Instead, the critical reader evaluates the evidence presented by the author in support of the claim. This is precisely what Chief Justice Warren does in his decision on the *Brown* case. Part of the evidence presented to the Court was a precedent, the 1896 *Plessy v. Ferguson* case in which separate facilities were ruled not inherently unequal. In evaluating the legitimacy of that evidence, Warren (speaking for the majority) notes that the nature and purposes of public education differ profoundly in 1896 and 1954 and that psychologists have in the meantime identified the negative impact of unequal treatment. Thus the *Plessy* case is not deemed a legitimate precedent, and it is rejected as grounds. While it may not be easy to determine the legitimacy of grounds or warrants in the arguments you read, you can measure them against the grounds you offer for your own position as well as those offered by people making opposing claims.

It is worth noting that you can reject the grounds and warrant in an argument without rejecting the claim itself. Many of us have been in the position of agreeing with a certain claim but bemoaning the fact that the grounds are insufficient to support it. You may support capital punishment, for example, but find unconvincing the argument that asks how you would feel if you were directly affected by a capital crime. Your judgment will not reflect your position on the issue, only your evaluation of the evidence. It is always wise to distinguish between your agreement with a claim and your evaluation of the legitimacy of the grounds.

Considering Alternative Perspectives

Because a published argument is usually designed to further the dialogue about a certain issue, you should consider reading alternative arguments in order to assess the effectiveness of the original argument you have read. It is only after considering an issue from multiple perspectives that you can consider yourself truly capable of taking a position on that issue. For Chief Justice Warren, of course, it was necessary to consider alternative arguments; his job (and the job of his colleagues on the Supreme Court) was to examine the grounds for a number of different claims regarding segregated schools. After reading "Graduation," you might consider alternative perspectives on one of the responses to segregation, affirmative action. In the past three decades affirmative action has come under fire not only from white conservatives but from black activists as well. While writers such as Henry Louis Gates and Orlando Patterson have written extensively about the value of affirmative action, it has been criticized by writers such as Shelby Steele and Dinesh D'Souza. Perhaps the most valuable result of reading alternative perspectives on an issue is the realization that few issues lend themselves to only two opposing positions. More often than not, a number of positions between the two extremes exist as well, and they can enlighten readers to the complexity of most arguments.

Once you have established an understanding of the topic, evaluated the evidence, and considered alternative perspectives, you should be prepared to respond to the argument. If that response is to take the form of a formal essay, then the following guidelines should be helpful.

Writing Arguments

Writing argumentative essays is not entirely different from writing other types of essays. Indeed, argumentative essays often employ narrative, definition, cause-and-effect, and other rhetorical strategies. The writing process itself is similar as well: You will engage in prewriting, composing, revising, and editing—just as you do in all of your formal writing. Argumentative essays, however, involve a more refined process of writing. Just as in reading arguments, in writing them you must understand the topic, evaluate the evidence, and consider alternative perspectives. In writing arguments, you engage in the same specific activities associated with reading arguments critically:

> **Understanding the topic**: Read extensively about the issue and develop your own claim.

> **Evaluating the evidence**: Determine what evidence supports your claim and decide upon an organizational strategy.

> **Considering alternative perspectives**: Identify the most convincing arguments in opposition to your claim and address them.

Understanding the Topic

If you are to write a convincing argument on any topic, you must be familiar with the issues involved. While you may be able to engage in informal debate about a topic, it is unlikely that you can compose a well supported essay without doing some formal research. Reading newspaper articles, editorial columns, letters to the editor, and magazine pieces; talking with representatives of organizations involved in the issue; and attending relevant meetings will help you to familiarize yourself with the multiple perspectives from which the issue can be considered. Just as Chief Justice Warren had to review a number of precedents before writing his decision in *Brown v. Board of Education*, you must become familiar with the background of your topic before writing your argument. It is even conceivable that you may change your position on the issue after researching it. Regardless of whether your research alters or solidifies your position, however, your task once you have completed your preliminary review of the issue is to develop a claim, or thesis, that you think is defensible.

For the purposes of this discussion, consider the following scenario: A toxic waste dump has been proposed for your community. After investigating the impact such facilities have had on other communities, you either oppose or support its construction. This example not only taps into a heated current debate, but it also involves issues of health, the environment, and economics, thus offering the opportunity to support the claim (whether in opposition to or in support of the dump) from a number of different perspectives. One possible thesis on this topic is the following:

> **Thesis:** Because of its impact on the economy, health, and the environment, a toxic waste dump should not be built in this community.

Whether or not you open your essay with the explicitly stated claim is a decision that should wait until later; it is normally best to concentrate on developing the argument itself before considering how to present it to your audience.

At this point, however, it is important to remember that failure to understand your audience can undermine an otherwise strong argument. As mentioned earlier, it is essential to recognize the needs and values of the audience as you compose your argument; remember, the most basic goal of argument is to convince the audience of the legitimacy of a claim. Thus the advice offered previously is worth repeating: Some audiences will be entirely sympathetic to your position, some will be antithetic, and many will fall somewhere between those two extremes. Your task in making an argument is to appeal to the **beliefs** and **values** of your audience. If you can find common beliefs and values, your task will be easier. For example, most members of a community will be sensitive to the economic impact of a toxic waste dump; a facility providing both jobs and tax dollars is an attractive prospect. You will be more persuasive, then, if you can address economic concerns. Perhaps you might balance the economic advantages of a dump with the increased costs of health care, loss of work due to illness, and decline of property values in order to appeal to those whose position stems from their sense of economic values.

Evaluating the Evidence

The evidence you choose to ground your argument depends not only on the nature of the claim itself but also on the needs and values of your audience. For example, if your community has demonstrated environmental awareness through recycling programs and conservation of land, then the environmental argument will be particularly appealing to them. If the community normally considers economic issues of primary importance, then the economic impact of the dump should be emphasized. Maya Angelou's audience is one that appreciates human-interest stories—her book is a memoir. Thus her appeal in "Graduation" is an emotional one, unlike Chief Justice Warren's rational appeal aimed at a legal audience. The nature and presentation of your evidence will also depend on your audience.

Suppose that you have determined from your reading on the subject and your knowledge of the people in the community that while economic issues are important to them, their primary concerns involve health and the environment. The following evidence, then, would be appropriate:

Evidence: Toxic waste dumps have been known to pollute the environment.

Increases in serious illnesses, including cancer, have been associated with toxic waste dumps.

Communities in which toxic waste dumps have been built have experienced a decline in property values and a loss of businesses.

In order to convince your audience of the legitimacy of this evidence, you will have to provide information such as examples of communities in which toxic waste dumps have been built, the opinion of experts on the relationship between the dumps and disease, and analyses of the economic impact of the dumps. The strength of your argument will depend in large part on how effectively you present this material. Pages of statistics with little narrative to break them up, for example, will likely confuse or bore all but the most technical audiences. Failure to make your warrant clear also will result in an unconvincing argument. While it is hardly necessary to state explicitly that the community values health, the environment, and a sound economic base, it will be necessary to establish the relative value of each of these features to a community. If you evaluate your evidence as conscientiously as you would that of an argument you were reading, your argument should be sound.

Considering Alternative Perspectives

When you are reading an argument, you consider alternative perspectives in order to evaluate the argument's effectiveness and to gauge your response to it. When writing an argument, you consider the opposition in order to strengthen your presentation. If you have conducted thorough research prior to making your claim, you should be aware of the alternative perspectives that might challenge you. Because of the significance of precedent in supporting a legal argument, for example, Chief Justice Warren addresses the *Plessy v. Ferguson* case explicitly in his argument, rebutting *Plessy's* claim by discussing the altered nature of public schools. You may have discovered evidence that toxic waste dumps bring needed tax revenues and jobs to the communities in which they are situated. If you are to argue successfully against the dump, you must address this evidence. If you can point to a decline in property values and a loss of other small businesses, then you have effectively countered the impact of the evidence.

Opposing view:	Dumps are an economic boon to communities because they generate tax revenues and increase employment.
Acknowledgment/ Rebuttal:	While dumps do provide taxes and jobs, their positive economic impact is mitigated by a decline in property values and a loss of other businesses.

What happens, however, if you do not have sufficient evidence to refute the economic claim? In this case, it will probably be necessary to revise your evidence to emphasize only health and environment, and to acknowledge that while dumps do have positive economic impact, their overall negative impact is more significant:

Opposing view:	Dumps are an economic boon to communities because they generate tax revenues and increase employment.

Acknowledgment/
Rebuttal: While dumps are economically valuable to a community, their negative impact on environment and health outweighs any economic benefits.

Whether you acknowledge alternative perspectives or rebut them, including them in your argument reveals not only that you are well versed in the subject, but also that you are fair-minded.

Composing the Paper

Once you have a clear idea of your position and the evidence you will use to support it, you can determine how to present your argument to your audience. At this stage you can rely on what you have learned about writing essays in general, using a few tips related specifically to argumentative writing.

Drafting an Introduction/Statement of Thesis

A variety of options exist for introducing an argument. You may want to begin with an anecdote, a brief story that engages your audience. You may want to begin with a statement of your thesis, establishing from the first sentence that you take this issue seriously. You may choose to use your introduction to establish the background of the issue and save your thesis until the essay's conclusion, after presenting evidence in favor of your position. These decisions will depend in large part on your audience. If your audience includes families in the community, for example, a well-chosen anecdote may drive home to them the real impact the dump will have on their lives. If the audience is less personally involved in the issue, however, you may choose to simply state your position. And if you want to persuade your audience without their necessarily being aware of it, you can wait until the end to state your claim, bringing the audience to your conclusion through your presentation.

Your introduction also depends on the nature of the subject and the argument itself. It may be necessary, for example, to define terms in your introduction, or to provide background information that may not be familiar to your audience. If the subject is particularly controversial, it may be necessary to acknowledge the legitimacy of various alternative perspectives before beginning the argument.

Deciding how to introduce the argument is not simply a stylistic decision. The effectiveness of the argument itself will be influenced by the way in which it is introduced.

Organizing the Evidence
Since it is the evidence that ultimately convinces most audiences, the decision on how to organize that evidence is a crucial one. As in determining how to introduce the argument, audience considerations are important. An unfriendly audience may need to be led step-by-step to your conclusion. In that case, you may want to begin with the least significant item of evidence and move to the most significant. This strategy assumes that if you can convince your audience to agree with you in small increments, then the audience will have no choice but to accept your claim at the end. Of course, the decision on how significant any piece of evidence is rests with the audience. A community overwhelmingly concerned with a high unemployment rate, for example, may consider the economic implications of a toxic waste dump far more significant than any long-term environmental impact. Moving from the environmental to the health and then to the economic evidence might be the most effective organizational strategy for this audience.

If your evidence includes something especially compelling, you may want to reverse this organization and start with the strongest piece of evidence. Suppose your evidence includes a report from a prestigious university indicating that the groundwater within several miles of every toxic waste dump built in the past decade has become contaminated. This evidence may be so powerful that you want to present it to your audience first, placing the rest of your evidence in a supporting role to this, the star witness. The advantage of such an organizational strategy is that you all but convince your audience with your first piece of evidence, making it easier for them to accept your other, less compelling evidence.

What do you do if the opposite is true? If there is a particularly strong opposing argument, you may wish to deal with that argument first. If you delay your rebuttal until you have presented your own evidence, you may have already lost your audience. It is possible that your audience will read your entire argument distracted by their curiosity about how you will deal with the opposition. Thus it is sometimes wise to present the opposing argument first, acknowledging its legitimacy, and then refuting its claims before moving on to your own evidence. The advantage of this approach is that you clear your audience's minds of distraction at the same time that you present yourself as a fair-minded person.

If you keep in mind both the audience and the nature of your evidence as you determine your organizational strategy, you should be able to construct a solid foundation on which to base your claim.

Concluding

A conventional conclusion to an argumentative paper will sum up the evidence and reinforce the thesis. If you have chosen to save your thesis for the end of the paper, however, the thesis will be stated explicitly for the first time in the conclusion. Other alternatives include returning to an anecdote used in the introduction, perhaps by completing the story based on the evidence you have amassed. You also may wish to issue a call to action in your conclusion. If you believe that your audience has been convinced, for example, that the toxic waste dump should not be built in the community, you may conclude with a call to join the movement opposing the dump. Whether you sum up, state the thesis for the first time, complete an anecdote, or issue a call to action, you want to make sure that your conclusion leaves your audience thinking seriously about your position—if not convinced that it is the right position.

Revising and Editing

The guidelines for revising a written argument are essentially the same as those for any other kind of paper: make sure that the thesis is clear, whether explicitly stated or implied; make sure that the organization is coherent and the evidence sound; and make sure that the conclusion is consistent and forceful. In particular, in revising an argumentative paper you should ask yourself the following questions:

1. Is your thesis clear, your position evident?

2. Is the audience provided with sufficient background on the topic?

3. Are all relevant terms defined?

4. Is the relevance of each item of evidence to the thesis made clear?

5. Are all underlying assumptions identified?

6. Are opposing views acknowledged and satisfactorily rebutted?

7. Is the organization of evidence effective?

8. Is the conclusion forceful and consistent with the thesis and evidence?

When you are ready to edit your paper, remember the earlier discussion of *pathos*. The effectiveness of your argument depends in part on the audience's perception of you as author. One of the surest and easiest ways to undermine your effectiveness is to ignore mechanical, grammatical, spelling, and format issues. At best your audience will be distracted by errors; at worst they will question the credibility of a writer either unwilling or unable to conform to the most basic conventions of standard written English. While it is obviously the argument itself that convinces the audience, a carefully edited paper will tell your audience that you not only care about your topic, but that you are a competent writer as well.

BIBLIOGRAPHY

Brockreide, Wayne, and Douglas Ehninger. "Toulmin on Argument: An Interpretation and Application." *The Quarterly Journal of Speech* 46 (1960): 44–53.

Fahnestock, Jeanne, and Marie Secor. "Teaching Argument: A Theory of Types. *College Composition and Communication* 34 (1983): 20–30.

Kaufer, David S., and Christine M. Neuwirth. "Integrating Formal Logic and the New Rhetoric: A Four-Stage Heuristic." *College English* 45 (1983): 380–389.

Kneupper, Charles W. "Teaching Argument: An Introduction to the Toulmin Model." *College Composition and Communication* 29 (1978): 237–241.

Toulmin, Stephen. *The Uses of Argument*. New York: Cambridge UP, 1964.

_____, Richard Rieke, and Allan Janik. *An Introduction to Reasoning*. New York: Macmillan, 1979.

Winder, Barbara E. "The Delineation of Values in Persuasive Writing." *College Composition and Communication* 29 (1978): 55–58.

Graduation

Maya Angelou

Maya Angelou (1928–) was born in St. Louis, Missouri, with the name Marguerite Johnson, but grew up with her grandmother in Stamps, Arkansas, from the age of 3. Her traumatic childhood included being raped at age 8 by her mother's boyfriend, after which she became mute for five years. She was shuttled back and forth between mother and grandmother, living for a brief time also with her father and running away to join a group of homeless children. At age 16 she gave birth to her son, Guy. She went through many life changes in the decades that followed, including success as a dancer and actor as well as experiences as a cook, a prostitute, and a chauffeur. Increasingly she focused on her writing, which includes four books of poetry and four plays, as well as the five autobiographical novels for which she is best known: I Know Why the Caged Bird Sings *(1970),* Gather Together in My Name *(1974),* Singin' and Swingin' and Gettin' Merry Like Christmas *(1976),* The Heart of a Woman *(1981), and* All God's Children Need Traveling Shoes *(1986). Angelou is an influential African-American author who has received many honors and fellowships. The essay "Graduation" is excerpted from* I Know Why the Caged Bird Sings, *which describes her early childhood. This essay focuses on the period in her life when she was learning what it meant to be black in a world dominated by whites, where discrimination affected not only her school but her whole world.*

From *I Know Why the Caged Bird Sings*. Published by Random House, Inc. Copyright © 1969 by Maya Angelou.

The children in Stamps trembled visibly with anticipation. Some adults were excited too, but to be certain the whole young population had come down with graduation epidemic. Large classes were graduating from both the grammar school and the high school. Even those who were years removed from their own day of glorious release were anxious to help with preparations as a kind of dry run. The junior students who were moving into the vacating classes' chairs were tradition-bound to show their talents for leadership and management. They strutted through the school and around the campus exerting pressure on the lower grades. Their authority was so new that occasionally if they pressed a little too hard it had to be overlooked. After all, next term was coming, and it never hurt a sixth-grader to have a play sister in the eighth grade, or a tenth-year student to be able to call a twelfth-grader Bubba. So all was endured in a spirit of shared understanding. But the graduating classes themselves were the nobility. Like travelers with exotic destinations on their minds, the graduates were remarkably forgetful. They came to school without their books, or tablets or even pencils. Volunteers fell over themselves to secure replacements for the missing equipment. When accepted, the willing workers might or might not be thanked, and it was of no importance to the pregraduation rites. Even teachers were respectful of the now quiet and aging seniors, and tended to speak to them, if not as equals, as beings only slightly lower than themselves. After tests were returned and grades given, the student body, which acted like an extended family, knew who did well, who excelled, and what piteous ones had failed.

Unlike the white high school, Lafayette County Training School distinguished itself by having neither lawn, nor hedges, nor tennis court, nor climbing ivy. Its two buildings (main classrooms, the grade school and home economics) were set on a dirt hill with no fence to limit either its boundaries or those of bordering farms. There was a large expanse to the left of the school which was used alternately as a baseball diamond or a basketball court. Rusty hoops on the swaying poles represented the permanent recreational equipment, although bats and balls could be borrowed from the P.E. teacher if the borrower was qualified and if the diamond wasn't occupied.

Over this rocky area relieved by a few shady tall persimmon trees the graduating class walked. The girls often held hands and no longer bothered to speak to the lower students. There was a sadness about them, as if this old world was not their home and they were bound for higher ground. The boys, on the other hand, had become more friendly, more outgoing. A decided change from the closed attitude they projected while studying for finals. Now they seemed not ready to give up the old school, the familiar paths and classrooms. Only a small percentage would be continuing on to college—one of the South's A & M (agricultural and mechanical) schools, which trained Negro youths to be carpenters, farmers, handymen, masons, maids, cooks and baby nurses. Their future rode heavily on their shoulders, and blinded them to the collective joy that had pervaded the lives of the boys and girls in the grammar school graduating class.

Parents who could afford it had ordered new shoes and ready-made clothes for themselves from Sears, Roebuck or Montgomery Ward. They also engaged the best seamstresses to make the floating graduating dresses and to cut down secondhand pants which would be pressed to a military slickness for the important event.

Oh, it was important, all right. Whitefolks would attend the ceremony, and two or three would speak of God and home, and the Southern way of life, and Mrs. Parsons, the principal's wife, would play the graduation march while the lower-grade graduates paraded down the aisles and took their seats below the platform. The high school seniors would wait in empty classrooms to make their dramatic entrance.

In the Store I was the person of the moment. The birthday girl. The center. Bailey had graduated the year before, although to do so he had had to forfeit all pleasures to make up for his time lost in Baton Rouge.

My class was wearing butter-yellow piqué dresses, and Momma launched out on mine. She smocked the yoke into tiny crisscrossing puckers, then shirred the rest of the bodice. Her dark fingers ducked in and out of the lemony cloth as she embroidered raised daisies around the hem. Before she considered herself finished she had added a crocheted cuff on the puff sleeves, and a pointy crocheted collar.

I was going to be lovely. A walking model of all the various styles of fine hand sewing and it didn't worry me that I was only twelve years old and merely graduating from the eighth grade. Besides, many teachers in Arkansas Negro schools had only that diploma and were licensed to impart wisdom.

The days had become longer and more noticeable. The faded beige of former times had been replaced with strong and sure colors. I began to see my classmates' clothes, their skin tones, and the dust that waved off pussy willows. Clouds that lazed across the sky were objects of great concern to me. Their shiftier shapes might have held a message that in my new happiness and with a little bit of time I'd soon decipher. During that period I looked at the arch of heaven so religiously my neck kept a steady ache. I had taken to smiling more often, and my jaws hurt from the unaccustomed activity. Between the two physical sore spots, I suppose I could have been uncomfortable, but that was not the case. As a member of the winning team (the graduating class of 1940) I had outdistanced unpleasant sensations by miles. I was headed for the freedom of open fields.

Youth and social approval allied themselves with me and we trammeled memories of slights and insults. The wind of our swift passage remodeled my features. Lost tears were pounded to mud and then to dust. Years of withdrawal were brushed aside and left behind, as hanging ropes of parasitic moss.

My work alone had awarded me a top place and I was going to be one of the first called in the graduating ceremonies. On the classroom blackboard, as well as on the bulletin board in the auditorium, there were blue stars and white stars and red stars. No absences, no tardinesses, and my academic work was among the best of the year. I could say the preamble to the Constitution even faster than Bailey. We timed ourselves often: "WethepeopleoftheUnitedStatesinordertoformamore perfectunion . . . " I had memorized the Presidents of the United States from Washington to Roosevelt in chronological as well as alphabetical order.

My hair pleased me too. Gradually the black mass had lengthened and thickened, so that it kept at last to its braided pattern, and I didn't have to yank my scalp off when I tried to comb it.

Louise and I had rehearsed the exercises until we tired out ourselves. Henry Reed was class valedictorian. He was a small, very black boy with hooded eyes, a long, broad nose and an oddly shaped head. I had admired him for years because each term he and I vied for the best grades in our class. Most often he bested me, but instead of being disappointed I was pleased that we shared top places between us. Like many Southern Black children, he lived with his grandmother, who was as strict as Momma and as kind as she knew how to be. He was courteous, respectful, and soft-spoken to elders, but on the playground he chose to play the roughest games. I admired him. Anyone, I reckoned, sufficiently afraid or sufficiently dull could be polite. But to be able to operate at a top level with both adults and children was admirable.

His valedictory speech was entitled "To Be or Not to Be." The rigid tenth-grade teacher had helped him write it. He'd been working on the dramatic stresses for months.

The weeks until graduation were filled with heady activities. A group of small children were to be presented in a play about buttercups and daisies and bunny rabbits. They could be heard throughout the building practicing their hops and their little songs that sounded like silver bells. The older girls (nongraduates, of course) were assigned the task of making refreshments for the night's festivities. A tangy scent of ginger, cinnamon, nutmeg and chocolate wafted around the home economics building as the budding cooks made samples for themselves and their teachers.

In every corner of the workshop, axes and saws split fresh timber as the woodshop boys made sets and stage scenery. Only the graduates were left out of the general bustle. We were free to sit in the library at the back of the building or look in quite detachedly, naturally, on the measures being taken for our event.

Even the minister preached on graduation the Sunday before. His subject was, "Let your light so shine that men will see your good works and praise your Father, Who is in Heaven." Although the sermon was purported to be addressed to us, he used the occasion to speak to backsliders, gamblers, and general ne'er-do-wells. But since he had called our names at the beginning of the service we were mollified.

Among Negroes the tradition was to give presents to children going only from one grade to another. How much more important this was when the person was graduating at the top of the class. Uncle Willie and Momma had sent away for a Mickey Mouse watch like Bailey's. Louise gave me four embroidered handkerchiefs. (I gave her three crocheted doilies.) Mrs. Sneed, the minister's wife, made me an underskirt to wear for graduation, and nearly every customer gave me a nickel or maybe even a dime with the instruction "Keep on moving to higher ground," or some such encouragement.

Amazingly the great day finally dawned and I was out of bed before I knew it. I threw open the back door to see it more clearly, but Momma said, "Sister, come away from that door and put your robe on."

I hoped the memory of that morning would never leave me. Sunlight was itself still young, and the day had none of the insistence maturity would bring it in a few hours. In my robe and barefoot in the backyard, under cover of going to see about my new beans, I gave myself up to the gentle warmth and thanked God that no matter what evil I had done in my life He had allowed me to live to see this day. Somewhere in my fatalism I had expected to die, accidentally, and never have the chance to walk up the stairs in the auditorium and gracefully receive my hard-earned diploma. Out of God's merciful bosom I had won reprieve.

Bailey came out in his robe and gave me a box wrapped in Christmas paper. He said he had saved his money for months to pay for it. It felt like a box of chocolates, but I knew Bailey wouldn't save money to buy candy when we had all we could want under our noses.

He was as proud of the gift as I. It was a soft-leatherbound copy of a collection of poems by Edgar Allan Poe, or, as Bailey and I called him, "Eap." I turned to "Annabel Lee" and we walked up and down the garden rows, the cool dirt between our toes, reciting the beautifully sad lines.

Momma made a Sunday breakfast although it was only Friday. After we finished the blessing, I opened my eyes to find the watch on my plate. It was a dream of a day. Everything went smoothly and to my credit. I didn't have to be reminded or scolded for anything. Near evening I was too jittery to attend to chores, so Bailey volunteered to do all before his bath.

Days before, we had made a sign for the Store, and as we turned out the lights Momma hung the cardboard over the doorknob. It read clearly: CLOSED. GRADUATION.

My dress fitted perfectly and everyone said that I looked like a sunbeam in it. On the hill, going toward the school, Bailey walked behind with Uncle Willie, who muttered, "Go on, Ju." He wanted him to walk ahead with us because it embarrassed him to have to walk so slowly. Bailey said he'd let the ladies walk together, and the men would bring up the rear. We all laughed, nicely.

Little children dashed by out of the dark like fireflies. Their crepe-paper dresses and butterfly wings were not made for running and we heard more than one rip, dryly, and the regretful "uh uh" that followed.

The school blazed without gaiety. The windows seemed cold and unfriendly from the lower hill. A sense of ill-fated timing crept over me, and if Momma hadn't reached for my hand I would have drifted back to Bailey and Uncle Willie, and possibly beyond. She made a few slow jokes about my feet getting cold, and tugged me along to the now-strange building.

Around the front steps, assurance came back. There were my fellow "greats," the graduating class. Hair brushed back, legs oiled, new dresses and pressed pleats, fresh pocket handkerchiefs and little handbags, all homesewn. Oh, we were up to snuff, all right. I joined my comrades and didn't even see my family go in to find seats in the crowded auditorium.

The school band struck up a march and all classes filed in as had been rehearsed. We stood in front of our seats, as assigned, and on a signal from the choir director, we sat. No sooner had this been accomplished than the band started to play the national anthem. We rose again and sang the song, after which we recited the pledge of allegiance. We remained standing for a brief minute before the choir director and the principal signaled to us, rather desperately I thought, to take our seats. The command was so unusual that our carefully rehearsed and smooth-running machine was thrown off. For a full minute we fumbled for our chairs and bumped into each other awkwardly. Habits change or solidify under pressure, so in our state of nervous tension we had been ready to follow our usual assembly pattern: the American national anthem, then the pledge of allegiance, then the song every Black person I knew called the Negro National Anthem. All done in the same key, with the same passion and most often standing on the same foot.

Finding my seat at last, I was overcome with a presentiment of worse things to come. Something unrehearsed, unplanned, was going to happen, and we were going to be made to look bad. I distinctly remember being explicit in the choice of pronoun. It was "we," the graduating class, the unit, that concerned me then.

The principal welcomed "parents and friends" and asked the Baptist minister to lead us in prayer. His invocation was brief and punchy, and for a second I thought we were getting back on the high road to right action. When the principal came back to the dais, however, his voice had changed. Sounds always affected me profoundly and the principal's voice was one of my favorites. During assembly it melted and lowed weakly into the audience. It had not been in my plan to listen to him, but my curiosity was piqued and I straightened up to give him my attention.

He was talking about Booker T. Washington, our "late great leader," who said we can be as close as the fingers on the hand, etc. . . . Then he said a few vague things about friendship and the friendship of kindly people to those less fortunate than themselves. With that his voice nearly faded, thin, away. Like a river diminishing to a stream and then to a trickle. But he cleared his throat and said, "Our speaker tonight, who is also our friend, came from Texarkana to deliver the commencement address, but due to the irregularity of the train schedule, he's going to, as they say, 'speak and run.' " He said that we understood and wanted the man to know that we were most grateful for the time he was able to give us and then something about how we were willing always to adjust to another's program, and without more ado—"I give you Mr. Edward Donleavy."

Not one but two white men came through the door offstage. The shorter one walked to the speaker's platform, and the tall one moved over to the center seat and sat down. But that was our principal's seat, and already occupied. The dislodged gentleman bounced around for a long breath or two before the Baptist minister gave him his chair, then with more dignity than the situation deserved, the minister walked off the stage.

Donleavy looked at the audience once (on reflection, I'm sure that he wanted only to reassure himself that we were really there), adjusted his glasses and began to read from a sheaf of papers.

He was glad "to be here and to see the work going on just as it was in the other schools."

At the first "Amen" from the audience I willed the offender to immediate death by choking on the word. But Amens and Yes, sir's began to fall around the room like rain through a ragged umbrella.

He told us of the wonderful changes we children in Stamps had in store. The Central School (naturally, the white school was Central) had already been granted improvements that would be in use in the fall. A well-known artist was coming from Little Rock to teach art to them. They were going to have the newest microscopes and chemistry equipment for their laboratory. Mr. Donleavy didn't leave us long in the dark over who made these improvements available to Central High. Nor were we to be ignored in the general betterment scheme he had in mind.

He said that he had pointed out to people at a very high level that one of the first-line football tacklers at Arkansas Agricultural and Mechanical College had graduated from good old Lafayette County Training School. Here fewer Amen's were heard. Those few that did break through lay dully in the air with the heaviness of habit.

He went on to praise us. He went on to say how he had bragged that "one of the best basketball players at Fisk sank his first ball right here at Lafayette County Training School."

The white kids were going to have a chance to become Galileos and Madame Curies and Edisons and Gauguins, and our boys (the girls weren't even in on it) would try to be Jesse Owenses and Joe Louises.

Owens and the Brown Bomber were great heroes in our world, but what school official in the white-goddom of Little Rock had the right to decide that those two men must be our only heroes? Who decided that for Henry Reed to become a scientist he had to work like George Washington Carver, as a bootblack, to buy a lousy microscope? Bailey was obviously always going to be too small to be an athlete, so which concrete angel glued to what country seat had decided that if my brother wanted to become a lawyer he had to first pay penance for his skin by picking cotton and hoeing corn and studying correspondence books at night for twenty years?

The man's dead words fell like bricks around the auditorium and too many settled in my belly. Constrained by hard-learned manners I couldn't look behind me, but to my left and right the proud graduating class of 1940 had dropped their heads. Every girl in my row had found something new to do with her handkerchief. Some folded the tiny squares into love knots, some into triangles, but most were wadding them, then pressing them flat on their yellow laps.

On the dais, the ancient tragedy was being replayed. Professor Parsons sat, a sculptor's reject, rigid. His large, heavy body seemed devoid of will or willingness, and his eyes said he was no longer with us. The other teachers examined the flag (which was draped stage right) or their notes, or the windows which opened on our now-famous playing diamond.

Graduation, the hush-hush magic time of frills and gifts and congratulations and diplomas, was finished for me before my name was called. The accomplishment was nothing. The meticulous maps, drawn in three colors of ink, learning and spelling decasyllabic words, memorizing the whole of *The Rape of Lucrece*—it was for nothing. Donleavy had exposed us.

We were maids and farmers, handymen and washerwomen, and anything higher that we aspired to was farcical and presumptuous.

Then I wished that Gabriel Prosser and Nat Turner had killed all whitefolks in their beds and that Abraham Lincoln had been assassinated before the signing of the Emancipation Proclamation, and that Harriet Tubman had been killed by that blow on her head and Christopher Columbus had drowned in the *Santa María*.

It was awful to be Negro and have no control over my life. It was brutal to be young and already trained to sit quietly and listen to charges brought against my color with no chance of defense. We should all be dead. I thought I should like to see us all dead, one on top of the other. A pyramid of flesh with the whitefolks on the bottom, as the broad base, then the Indians with their silly tomahawks and teepees and wigwams and treaties, the Negroes with their mops and recipes and cotton sacks and spirituals sticking out of their mouths. The Dutch children should all stumble in their wooden shoes and break their necks. The French should choke to death on the Louisiana Purchase (1803) while silkworms ate all the Chinese with their stupid pigtails. As a species, we were an abomination. All of us.

Donleavy was running for election, and assured our parents that if he won we could count on having the only colored paved playing field in that part of Arkansas. Also—he never looked up to acknowledge the grunts of acceptance—also, we were bound to get some new equipment for the home economics building and the workshop.

He finished, and since there was no need to give any more than the most perfunctory thank-you's, he nodded to the men on the stage, and the tall white man who was never introduced joined him at the door. They left with the attitude that now they were off to something really important. (The graduation ceremonies at Lafayette Country Training School had been a mere preliminary.)

The ugliness they left was palpable. An uninvited guest who wouldn't leave. The choir was summoned and sang a modern arrangement of "Onward, Christian Soldiers," with new words pertaining to graduates seeking their place in the world. But it didn't work. Elouise, the daughter of the Baptist minister, recited "Invictus," and I could have cried at the impertinence of "I am the master of my fate, I am the captain of my soul."

My name had lost its ring of familiarity and I had to be nudged to go and receive my diploma. All my preparations had fled. I neither marched up to the stage like a conquering Amazon, nor did I look in the audience for Bailey's nod of approval. Marguerite Johnson, I heard the name again, my honors were read, there were noises in the audience of appreciation, and I took my place on the stage as rehearsed.

I thought about colors I hated: ecru, puce, lavender, beige and black.

There was shuffling and rustling around me, then Henry Reed was giving his valedictory address, "To Be or Not to Be." Hadn't he heard the whitefolks? We couldn't *be*, so the question was a waste of time. Henry's voice came out clear and strong. I feared to look at him. Hadn't he got the message? There was no "nobler in the mind" for Negroes because the world didn't think we had minds, and they let us know it. "Outrageous fortune"? Now, that was a joke. When the ceremony was over I had to tell Henry Reed some things. That is, if I still cared. Not "rub," Henry, "erase." "Ah, there's the erase." Us.

Henry had been a good student in elocution. His voice rose on tides of promise and fell on waves of warnings. The English teacher had helped him to create a sermon winging through Hamlet's soliloquy. To be a man, a doer, a builder, a leader, or to be a tool, an unfunny joke, a crusher of funky toadstools. I marveled that Henry could go through with the speech as if we had a choice.

I had been listening and silently rebutting each sentence with my eyes closed; then there was a hush, which in an audience warns that something unplanned is happening. I looked up and saw Henry Reed, the conservative, the proper, the A student, turn his back to the audience and turn to us (the proud graduating class of 1940) and sing, nearly speaking,

"Lift ev'ry voice and sing
Till earth and heaven ring
Ring with the harmonies of Liberty . . . "

It was the poem written by James Weldon Johnson. It was the music composed by J. Rosamond Johnson. It was the Negro national anthem. Out of habit we were singing it.

Our mothers and fathers stood in the dark hall and joined the hymn of encouragement. A kindergarten teacher led the small children onto the stage and the buttercups and daisies and bunny rabbits marked time and tried to follow:

"Stony the road we trod
Bitter the chastening rod
Felt in the days when hope, unborn, had died.
'Yet with a steady beat
Have not our weary feet
Come to the place for which our fathers sighed?"

Every child I knew had learned that song with his ABC's and along with "Jesus Loves Me This I Know." But I personally had never heard it before. Never heard the words, despite the thousands of times I had sung them. Never thought they had anything to do with me.

On the other hand, the words of Patrick Henry had made such an impression on me that I had been able to stretch myself tall and trembling and say, "I know not what course others may take, but as for me, give me liberty or give me death."

And now I heard, really for the first time:

"We have come over a way that with tears
has been watered,
We have come, treading our path through
the blood of the slaughtered."

While echoes of the song shivered in the air, Henry Reed bowed his head, said "Thank you," and returned to his place in the line. The tears that slipped down many faces were not wiped away in shame.

We were on top again. As always, again. We survived. The depths had been icy and dark, but now a bright sun spoke to our souls. I was no longer simply a member of the proud graduating class of 1940; I was a proud member of the wonderful, beautiful Negro race.

Oh, Black known and unknown poets, how often have your auctioned pains sustained us? Who will compute the lonely nights made less lonely by your songs, or the empty pots made less tragic by your tales?

If we were a people much given to revealing secrets, we might raise monuments and sacrifice to the memories of our poets, but slavery cured us of that weakness. It may be enough, however, to have it said that we survive in exact relationship to the dedication of our poets (include preachers, musicians and blues singers).

Of Studies

Francis Bacon

Francis Bacon (1561–1626) was born in London, studied at Trinity College, Cambridge, and trained for law at Gray's Inn. He served the courts of Queen Elizabeth and then King James I, was knighted in 1603, and was made a baron in 1618 and then a viscount in 1621. He was later accused of accepting bribes at court and was convicted and briefly imprisoned before being pardoned. Bacon is known both for his Essays or Counsels, Civil and Moral *and his discourses on the "new science" methods of inductive observation and experimentation. Interestingly, perhaps because he was often adept at turning a phrase, some have theorized (falsely, according to most critics) that Bacon is the true author of some of Shakespeare's plays. As perhaps the originator of the essay genre in English, Bacon was influenced by the French essayist Montaigne. "Of Studies" is typical of many of Bacon's essays as a brief exploration of an idea, described with a flourish of rhetoric and extended figures of speech. Modern readers are sometimes impatient with Bacon's style, but if you read the essay without haste you may find yourself appreciating the ebb and flow of his phrases. An interesting effect can be achieved by reading this essay aloud, with a slightly pompous tone, as if to a court or congregation.*

1   Studies serve for delight, for ornament, and for ability. Their chief use for delight is in privateness, and retiring; for ornament, is in discourse; and for ability, is in the judgment and disposition of business; for, expert men can execute, and perhaps judge of particulars, one by one; but the general counsels, and the plots and marshaling of affairs, come best from those that are learned. To spend too much time in studies, is sloth; to use them too much for ornament, is affectation; to make judgment wholly by their rules, is the humour of

a scholar; they perfect nature, and are perfected by experience—for natural abilities are like natural plants, that need pruning by study; and studies themselves do give forth directions too much at large, except they be bounded in by experience. Crafty men condemn studies, simple men admire them, and wise men use them, for they teach not their own use; but that is a wisdom without them, and above them, won by observation. Read not to contradict and confute nor to believe and take for granted, nor to find talk and discourse, but to weigh and consider. Some books are to be tasted, others to be swallowed, and some few to be chewed and digested; that is, some books are to be read only in parts; others to be read, but not curiously; and some few to be read wholly, and with diligence and attention. Some books also may be read by deputy, and extracts made of them by others; but that would be only in the less important arguments, and the meaner sort of books; else distilled books are, like common distilled waters, flashy things. Reading maketh a full man, conference a ready man, and writing an exact man; and, therefore, if a man write little, he had need have a great memory; if he confer little, he had need have a present wit; and if he read little, he had need have much cunning, to seem to know that he doth not. Histories make men wise; poets witty; the mathematics subtle; natural philosophy deep; moral, grave; logic and rhetoric, able to contend: *abeunt studia in mores.*—Nay, there is no stond or impediment in the wit, but may be wrought out by fit studies, like as diseases of the body may have appropriate exercises—bowling is good for the stone and reins, shooting for the lungs and breast, gentle walking for the stomach, riding for the head, and the like; so, if a man's wit be wandering, let him study the mathematics, for in demonstrations, if his wit be called away never so little, he must begin again; if his wit be not apt to distinguish or find differences, let him study the schoolmen, for they are *cymini sectores,* if he be not apt to beat over matters, and to call upon one thing to prove and illustrate another, let him study the lawyers' cases—so every defect of the mind may have a special receipt.

A Modest Proposal

Jonathan Swift

Born in Dublin, Ireland, Jonathan Swift (1667–1745) entered the clergy after his education at Trinity College and Oxford University. Through his long life he wrote in a wide range of genres, including poetry, religious pamphlets, essays, and satires on various social and political themes. His best-known work is Gulliver's Travels, *a combination of children's story and social satire. Swift was always a supporter of Irish causes, as can be seen in "A Modest Proposal," which was published anonymously in 1729. In this ironic essay, the speaker—the "I"—is not Swift himself but a persona, a fictional voice who gives his proposal to cure the ills of contemporary Ireland. It is true that Ireland at this time had the problems described by this persona: poverty, unemployment, a failing economy, exploitation by the wealthy classes, conflict between the Anglican and Catholic churches, and so on. This is the serious subject Swift addresses through his satire. If you have not read or heard of his "proposal" previously, read slowly and attentively: you might be greatly surprised to learn the nature of his proposition.*

1   It is a melancholy object to those who walk through this great town or travel in the country, when they see the streets, the roads, and cabin doors, crowded with beggars of the female sex, followed by three, four, or six children, all in rags and importuning every passenger for an alms. These mothers, instead of being able to work for their honest livelihood, are forced to employ all their time in strolling to beg sustenance for their helpless infants, who, as they grow up, either turn thieves for want of work, or leave their dear native country to fight for the Pretender in Spain, or sell themselves to the Barbadoes.

I think it is agreed by all parties that this prodigious number of children in the arms, or on the backs, or at the heels of their mothers, and frequently of their fathers, is in the present deplorable state of the kingdom a very great additional grievance; and therefore whoever could find out a fair, cheap, and easy method of making these children sound, useful members of the commonwealth would deserve so well of the public as to have his statue set up for a preserver of the nation.

But my intention is very far from being confined to provide only for the children of professed beggars; it is of a much greater extent, and shall take in the whole number of infants at a certain age who are born of parents in effect as little able to support them as those who demand our charity in the streets.

As to my own part, having turned my thoughts for many years upon this important subject, and maturely weighed the several schemes of other projectors, I have always found them grossly mistaken in their computation. It is true, a child just dropped from its dam may be supported by her milk for a solar year, with little other nourishment; at most not above the value of two shillings, which the mother may certainly get, or the value in scraps, by her lawful occupation of begging; and it is exactly at one year old that I propose to provide for them in such a manner as instead of being a charge upon their parents or the parish, or wanting food and raiment for the rest of their lives, they shall on the contrary contribute to the feeding, and partly to the clothing, of many thousands.

5   There is likewise another great advantage in my scheme, that it will prevent those voluntary abortions, and that horrid practice of women murdering their bastard children, alas, too frequent among us, sacrificing the poor innocent babes, I doubt, more to avoid the expense than the shame, which would move tears and pity in the most savage and inhuman breast.

The number of souls in this kingdom being usually reckoned one million and a half, of these I calculate there may be about two hundred thousand couples whose wives are breeders; from which number I subtract thirty thousand couples who are able to maintain their own children, although I apprehend there cannot be so many under the present distresses of the kingdom; but this being granted, there will remain an hundred and seventy thousand breeders. I again subtract fifty thousand for those women who miscarry, or whose children die by accident or disease within the year. There only remain an hundred and twenty thousand children of poor parents annually born. The question therefore is, how this number shall be reared and provided for, which, as I have already said, under the present situation of affairs, is utterly impossible by all the methods hitherto proposed. For we can neither employ them in handicraft nor agriculture; we neither build houses (I mean in the country) nor cultivate land. They can very seldom pick up livelihood by stealing till they arrive at six years old, except where they are of towardly parts; although I confess they learn the rudiments much earlier, during which time they can however be looked upon only as probationers, as I have been informed by a principal gentleman in the county of Cavan, who protested to me that he never knew above one or two instances under the age of six, even in a part of the kingdom so renowned for the quickest proficiency in that art.

I am assured by our merchants that a boy or a girl before twelve years old is no salable commodity; and even when they come to this age, they will not yield above three pounds, or three pounds and half a crown at most on the Exchange; which cannot turn to account either to the parents or the kingdom, the charge of nutriment and rags having been at least four times that value.

I shall now therefore humbly propose my own thoughts, which I hope will not be liable to the least objection.

I have been assured by a very knowing American of my acquaintance in London, that a young healthy child well nursed is at a year old a most delicious, nourishing, and wholesome food, whether stewed, roasted, baked, or boiled; and I make no doubt that it will equally serve in a fricassee or a ragout.

10   I do therefore humbly offer it to public consideration that of the   10 hundred and twenty thousand children, already computed, twenty thousand may be reserved for breed, whereof only one fourth part to be males, which is more than we allow to sheep, black cattle, or swine; and my reason is that these children are seldom the fruits of marriage, a circumstance not much regarded by our savages, therefore one male will be sufficient to serve four females. That the remaining hundred thousand may at a year old be offered in sale to the persons of quality and fortune through the kingdom, always advising the mother to let them suck plentifully in the last month, so as to render them plump and fat for a good table. A child will make two dishes at an entertainment for friends; and when the family dines alone, the fore or hind quarter will make a reasonable dish, and seasoned with a little pepper or salt will be very good boiled on the fourth day, especially in winter.

I have reckoned upon a medium that a child just born will weigh twelve pounds, and in a solar year if tolerably nursed increaseth to twenty-eight pounds.

I grant this food will be somewhat dear, and therefore very proper for landlords, who, as they have already devoured most of the parents, seem to have the best title to the children.

Infant's flesh will be in season throughout the year, but more plentiful in March, and a little before and after. For we are told by a grave author, an eminent French physician, that fish being a prolific diet, there are more children born in Roman Catholic countries about nine months after Lent, than at any other season; therefore, reckoning a year after Lent, the markets will be more glutted than usual, because the number of popish infants is at least three to one in this kingdom; and therefore it will have one other collateral advantage, by lessening the number of Papists among us.

I have already computed the charge of nursing a beggar's child (in which list I reckon all cottagers, laborers, and four fifths of the farmers) to be about two shillings per annum, rags included; and I believe no gentleman would repine to give ten shillings for the carcass of a good fat child, which, as I have said, will make four dishes of excellent nutritive meat, when he hath only some particular friend or his own family to dine with him. Thus the squire will learn to be a good landlord, and grow popular among the tenants; the mother will have eight shillings net profit, and be fit for work till she produces another child.

15 Those who are more thrifty (as I must confess the times require) 15 may flay the carcass; the skin of which artificially dressed will make admirable gloves for ladies, and summer boots for fine gentlemen.

As to our city of Dublin, shambles may be appointed for this purpose in the most convenient parts of it, and butchers we may be assured will not be wanting; although I rather recommend buying the children alive, and dressing them hot from the knife as we do roasting pigs.

A very worthy person, a true lover of his country, and whose virtues I highly esteem, was lately pleased in discoursing on this matter to offer a refinement upon my scheme. He said that many gentlemen of his kingdom, having of late destroyed their deer, he conceived that the want of venison might be well supplied by the bodies of young lads and maidens, not exceeding fourteen years of age nor under twelve, so great a number of both sexes in every county being now ready to starve for want of work and service; and these to be disposed of by their parents, if alive, or otherwise by their nearest relations. But with due deference to so excellent a friend and so deserving a patriot, I cannot be altogether in his sentiments; for as to the males, my American acquaintance assured me from frequent experience that their flesh was generally tough and lean, like that of our schoolboys, by continual exercise, and their taste disagreeable; and to fatten them would not answer the charge. Then as to the females, it would, I think with humble submission, be a loss to the public, because they soon would become breeders themselves; and besides, it is not improbable that some scrupulous people might be apt to censure such a practice (although indeed very unjustly) as a little bordering upon cruelty; which, I confess, hath always been with me the strongest objection against any project, how well soever intended.

But in order to justify my friend, he confessed that this expedient was put into his head by the famous Psalmanazar, a native of the island Formosa, who came from thence to London above twenty years ago, and in conversation told my friend that in his country when any young person happened to be put to death, the executioner sold the carcass to persons of quality as a prime dainty; and that in his time the body of a plump girl of fifteen, who was crucified for an attempt to poison the emperor, was sold to his Imperial Majesty's prime minister of state, and other great mandarins of the court, in joints from the gibbet, at four hundred crowns. Neither indeed can I deny that if the same use were made of several plump young girls in this town, who without one single groat to their fortunes cannot stir abroad without a chair, and appear at the playhouse and assemblies in foreign fineries which they never will pay for, the kingdom would not be the worse.

Some persons of a desponding spirit are in great concern about that vast number of poor people who are aged, diseased, or maimed, and I have been desired to employ my thoughts what course may be taken to ease the nation of so grievous an encumbrance. But I am not in the least pain upon that matter, because it is very well known that they are every day dying and rotting by cold and famine, and filth and vermin, as fast as can be reasonably expected. And as to the younger laborers, they are now in almost as hopeful a condition. They cannot get work, and consequently pine away for want of nourishment to a degree that if any time they are accidentally hired to common labor, they have not strength to perform it; and thus the country and themselves are happily delivered from the evils to come.

20   I have too long digressed, and therefore shall return to my subject. I think the advantages by the proposal which I have made are obvious and many, as well as of the highest importance.

For first, as I have already observed, it would greatly lessen the number of Papists, with whom we are yearly overrun, being the principal breeders of the nation as well as our most dangerous enemies; and who stay at home on purpose to deliver the kingdom to the Pretender, hoping to take their advantage by the absence of so many good Protestants, who have chosen rather to leave their country than to stay at home and pay tithes against their conscience to an Episcopal curate.

Secondly, the poorer tenants will have something valuable of their own, which by law may be made liable to distress, and help to pay their landlord's rent, their corn and cattle being already seized and money a thing unknown.

Thirdly, whereas the maintenance of an hundred thousand children, from two years old and upwards, cannot be computed at less than ten shillings a piece per annum, the nation's stock will be thereby increased fifty thousand pounds per annum, besides the profit of a new dish introduced to the tables of all gentlemen of fortune in the kingdom who have any refinement in taste. And the money will circulate among ourselves, the goods being entirely of our own growth and manufacture.

Fourthly, the constant breeders, besides the gain of eight shillings sterling per annum by the sale of their children, will be rid of the charge of maintaining them after the first year.

25   Fifthly, this food would likewise bring great custom to taverns, where the vintners will certainly be so prudent as to procure the best receipts for dressing it to perfection, and consequently have their houses frequented by all the fine gentlemen, who justly value themselves upon their knowledge in good eating; and a skillful cook, who understands how to oblige his guests, will contrive to make it as expensive as they please.

Sixthly, this would be a great inducement to marriage, which all wise nations have either encouraged by rewards or enforced by laws and penalties. It would increase the care and tenderness of mothers toward their children, when they were sure of a settlement for life to the poor babes, provided in some sort by the public, to their annual profit instead of expense. We should see an honest emulation among the married women, which of them could bring the fattest child to the market. Men would become as fond of their wives during the time of pregnancy as they are now of their mares in foal, their cows in calf, or sows when they are ready to farrow; nor offer to beat or kick them (as is too frequent a practice) for fear of a miscarriage.

Many other advantages might be enumerated. For instance, the addition of some thousand carcasses in our exportation of barreled beef, the propagation of swine's flesh, and improvement in the art of making good bacon, so much wanted among us by the great destruction of pigs, too frequent at our tables, which are no way comparable in taste or magnificence to a well-grown, fat, yearling child, which roasted whole will make a considerable figure at a lord mayor's feast or any other public entertainment. But this and many others I omit, being studious of brevity.

Supposing that one thousand families in this city would be constant customers for infants' flesh, besides others who might have it at merry meetings, particularly weddings and christenings, I compute that Dublin would take off annually about twenty thousand carcasses, and the rest of the kingdom (where probably they will be sold somewhat cheaper) the remaining eighty thousand.

I can think of no one objection that will possibly be raised against this proposal, unless it should be urged that the number of people will be thereby much lessened in the kingdom. This I freely own, and it was indeed one principal design in offering it to the world. I desire the reader will observe; that I calculate my remedy for this one individual kingdom of Ireland and for no other that ever was, is, or I think ever can be upon earth. Therefore, let no man talk to me of other expedients: of taxing our absentees at five shillings a pound: of using neither clothes nor household furniture except what is of our own growth and manufacture: of utterly rejecting the materials and instruments that promote foreign luxury: of curing the expensiveness of pride, vanity, idleness, and gaming in our women: of introducing a vein of parsimony, prudence, and temperance: of learning to love our country, in the want of which we differ even from Laplanders and the inhabitants of Topinamboo: of quitting our animosities and factions, nor acting any longer like the Jews, who were murdering one another at the very moment their city was taken: of being a little cautious not to sell our country and conscience for nothing: of teaching landlords to have at least one degree of mercy toward their tenants: lastly, of putting a spirit of honesty, industry, and skill into our shopkeepers; who, if a resolution could now be taken to buy only our native goods, would immediately unite to cheat and exact upon us in the price, the measure, and the goodness, nor could ever yet be brought to make one fair proposal of just dealing, though often and earnestly invited to it.

30   Therefore, I repeat, let no man talk to me of these and the like expedients, till he hath at least some glimpse of hope that there will ever be some hearty and sincere attempt to put them in practice. 30

But as to myself, having been wearied out for many years with offering vain, idle, visionary thoughts, and at length utterly despairing of success, I fortunately fell upon this proposal, which, as it is wholly new, so it hath something solid and real, of no expense and little trouble, full in our own power, and whereby we can incur no danger in disobliging England. For this kind of commodity will not bear exportation, the flesh being of too tender a consistence to admit a long continuance in salt, although perhaps I could name a country which would be glad to eat up our whole nation without it.

After all, I am not so violently bent upon my own opinion as to reject any offer proposed by wise men, which shall be found equally innocent, cheap, easy, and effectual. But before something of that kind shall be advanced in contradiction to my scheme, and offering a better, I desire the author or authors will be pleased maturely to consider two points. First, as things now stand, how they will be able to find food and raiment for an hundred thousand useless mouths and backs. And secondly, there being a round million of creatures in human figure throughout this kingdom, whose sole subsistence put into a common stock would leave them in debt two millions of pounds sterling, adding those who are beggars by profession to the bulk of farmers, cottagers, and laborers, with their wives and children who are beggars in effect; I desire those politicians who dislike my overture, and may perhaps be so bold to attempt an answer, that they will first ask the parents of these mortals whether they would not at this day think it a great happiness to have been sold for food at a year old in this manner I prescribe, and thereby have avoided such a perpetual scene of misfortunes as they have since gone through by the oppression of landlords, the impossibility of paying rent without money or trade, the want of common sustenance, with neither house nor clothes to cover them from the inclemencies of the weather, and the most inevitable prospect of entailing the like or greater miseries upon their breed forever.

I profess, in the sincerity of my heart, that I have not the least personal interest in endeavoring to promote this necessary work, having no other motive than the public good of my country, by advancing our trade, providing for infants, relieving the poor, and giving some pleasure to the rich. I have no children by which I can propose to get a single penny; the youngest being nine years old, and my wife past childbearing.

Once More to the Lake

E.B. White

E.B. White (1899–1985) was born in Mt. Vernon, New York, and attended Cornell University. He was a career writer of newspaper pieces and essays for the magazines The New Yorker *and* Harper's. *His three children's books have become classics:* Stuart Little, Charlotte's Web, *and* The Trumpet of the Swan. *As an accomplished stylist, he revised the grammar book by Strunk that he had himself used as a student—which is now known universally as Strunk and White's* Elements of Style. *The essay "Once More to the Lake" was originally published in White's* One Man's Meat *in 1941. It examines what seems to be White's idyllic childhood of summers at a lake in Maine, revisited decades later by an older White who at first seems nostalgic. The essay gives us much more, however, than wistful memories of a happy time in a beautiful place.*

1   One summer, along about 1904, my father rented a camp on   1
a lake in Maine and took us all there for the month of August. We all got ringworm from some kittens and had to rub Pond's Extract on our arms and legs night and morning, and my father rolled over in a canoe with all his clothes on; but outside of that the vacation was a success and from then on none of us ever thought there was any place in the world like that lake in Maine. We returned summer after summer—always on August 1st for one month. I have since become a salt-water man, but sometimes in summer there are days when the restlessness of the tides and the fearful cold of the sea water and the incessant wind which blows across the afternoon and into the evening make me wish for the placidity of a lake in the woods. A few weeks ago this feeling got so strong I bought myself a couple of

bass hooks and a spinner and returned to the lake where we used to go, for a week's fishing and to revisit old haunts.

I took along my son, who had never had any fresh water up his nose and who had seen lily pads only from train windows. On the journey over to the lake I began to wonder what it would be like. I wondered how time would have marred this unique, this holy spot— the coves and streams, the hills that the sun set behind, the camps and the paths behind the camps. I was sure the tarred road would have found it out, and I wondered in what other ways it would be desolated. It is strange how much you can remember about places like that once you allow your mind to return into the grooves which lead back. You remember one thing, and that suddenly reminds you of another thing. I guess I remembered clearest of all the early mornings, when the lake was cool and motionless, remembered how the bedroom smelled of the lumber it was made of and of the wet woods whose scent entered through the screen. The partitions in the camp were thin and did not extend clear to the top of the rooms, and as I was always the first up I would dress softly so as not to wake the others, and sneak out into the sweet outdoors and start out in the canoe, keeping close along the shore in the long shadows of the pines. I remembered being very careful never to rub my paddle against the gunwale for fear of disturbing the stillness of the cathedral.

The lake had never been what you would call a wild lake. There were cottages sprinkled around the shores, and it was in farming country although the shores of the lake were quite heavily wooded. Some of the cottages were owned by nearby farmers, and you would live at the shore and eat your meals at the farmhouse. That's what our family did. But although it wasn't wild, it was a fairly large and undisturbed lake and there were places in it which, to a child at least, seemed infinitely remote and primeval.

I was right about the tar: it led to within half a mile of the shore. But when I got back there, with my boy, and we settled into a camp near a farmhouse and into the kind of summertime I had known, I could tell that it was going to be pretty much the same as it had been before—I knew it, lying in bed the first morning, smelling the bedroom, and hearing the boy sneak quietly out and go off along the shore in a boat. I began to sustain the illusion that he was I, and therefore, by simple transposition, that I was my father. This sensation persisted, kept cropping up all the time we were there. It was not an entirely new feeling, but in this setting it grew much stronger. I seemed to be living a dual existence. I would be in the middle of some simple act, I would be picking up a bait box or laying down a table fork, or I would be saying something, and suddenly it would be not I but my father who was saying the words or making the gesture. It gave me a creepy sensation.

5   We went fishing the first morning. I felt the same damp moss covering the worms in the bait can, and saw the dragonfly alight on the tip of my rod as it hovered a few inches from the surface of the water. It was the arrival of this fly that convinced me beyond any doubt that everything was as it always had been, that the years were a mirage and there had been no years. The small waves were the same, chucking the rowboat under the chin as we fished at anchor, and the boat was the same boat, the same color green and the ribs broken in the same places, and under the floor-boards the same freshwater leavings and débris—the dead helgramite, the wisps of moss, the rusty discarded fishhook, the dried blood from yesterday's catch. We stared silently at the tips of our rods, at the dragonflies that came and went. I lowered the tip of mine into the water, tentatively, pensively dislodging the fly, which darted two feet away, poised, darted two feet back, and came to rest again a little farther up the rod. There had been no years between the ducking of this dragonfly and the other one—the one that was part of memory. I looked at the boy, who was silently watching his fly, and it was my hands that held his rod, my eyes watching. I felt dizzy and didn't know which rod I was at the end of.

We caught two bass, hauling them in briskly as though they were mackerel, pulling them over the side of the boat in a businesslike manner without any landing net, and stunning them with a blow on the back of the head. When we got back for a swim before lunch, the lake was exactly where we had left it, the same number of inches from the dock, and there was only the merest suggestion of a breeze. This seemed an utterly enchanted sea, this lake you could leave to its own devices for a few hours and come back to, and find that it had not stirred, this constant and trustworthy body of water. In the shallows, the dark, water-soaked sticks and twigs, smooth and old, were undulating in clusters on the bottom against the clean ribbed sand, and the track of the mussel was plain. A school of minnows swam by, each minnow with its small individual shadow, doubling the attendance, so clear and sharp in the sunlight. Some of the other campers were in swimming, along the shore, one of them with a cake of soap, and the water felt thin and clear and unsubstantial. Over the years there had been this person with the cake of soap, this cultist, and here he was. There had been no years.

Up to the farmhouse to dinner through the teeming, dusty field, the road under our sneakers was only a two-track road. The middle track was missing, the one with the marks of the hooves and the splotches of dried, flaky manure. There had always been three tracks to choose from in choosing which track to walk in; now the choice was narrowed down to two. For a moment I missed terribly the middle alternative. But the way led past the tennis court, and something about the way it lay there in the sun reassured me; the tape had loosened along the backline, the alleys were green with plantains and other weeds, and the net (installed in June and removed in September) sagged in the dry noon, and the whole place steamed with midday heat and hunger and emptiness. There was a choice of pie for dessert, and one was blueberry and one was apple, and the waitresses were the same country girls, there having been no passage of time, only the illusion of it as in a dropped curtain—the waitresses were still fifteen; their hair had been washed, that was the only difference—they had been to the movies and seen the pretty girls with the clean hair.

Summertime, oh summertime, pattern of life indelible, the fade-proof lake, the woods unshatterable, the pasture with the sweetfern and the juniper forever and ever, summer without end; this was the background, and the life along the shore was the design, the cottages with their innocent and tranquil design, their tiny docks with the flagpole and the American flag floating against the white clouds in the blue sky, the little paths over the roots of the trees leading from camp to camp and the paths leading back to the outhouses and the can of lime for sprinkling, and at the souvenir counters at the store the miniature birch-bark canoes and the post cards that showed things looking a little better than they looked. This was the American family at play, escaping the city heat, wondering whether the newcomers in the camp at the head of the cove were "common" or "nice," wondering whether it was true that the people who drove up for Sunday dinner at the farmhouse were turned away because there wasn't enough chicken.

It seemed to me, as I kept remembering all this, that those times and those summers had been infinitely precious and worth saving.

There had been jollity and peace and goodness. The arriving (at the beginning of August) had been so big a business in itself, at the railway station the farm wagon drawn up, the first smell of the pine-laden air, the first glimpse of the smiling farmer, and the great importance of the trunks and your father's enormous authority in such matters, and the feel of the wagon under you for the long ten-mile haul, and at the top of the last long hill catching the first view of the lake after eleven months of not seeing this cherished body of water. The shouts and cries of the other campers when they saw you, and the trunks to be unpacked, to give up their rich burden. (Arriving was less exciting nowadays, when you sneaked up in your car and parked it under a tree near the camp and took out the bags and in five minutes it was all over, no fuss, no loud wonderful fuss about trunks.)

10   Peace and goodness and jollity. The only thing that was wrong   10
now, really, was the sound of the place, an unfamiliar nervous sound of the outboard motors. This was the note that jarred, the one thing that would sometimes break the illusion and set the years moving. In those other summertimes all motors were inboard; and when they were at a little distance, the noise they made was a sedative, an ingredient of summer sleep. They were one-cylinder and two-cylinder engines, and some were make-and-break and some were jump-spark, but they all made a sleepy sound across the lake. The one-lungers throbbed and fluttered, and the twin-cylinder ones purred and purred, and that was a quiet sound too. But now the campers all had outboards. In the daytime, in the hot mornings, these motors made a petulant, irritable sound; at night, in the still evening when the afterglow lit the water, they whined about one's ears like mosquitoes. My boy loved our rented outboard, and his great desire was to achieve singlehanded mastery over it, and authority, and he soon learned the trick of choking it a little (but not too much), and the adjustment of the needle valve. Watching him I would remember the things you could do with the old one-cylinder engine with the heavy flywheel, how you could have it eating out of your hand if you got really close to it spiritually. Motor boats in those days didn't have clutches, and you would make a landing by shutting off the motor at the proper time and coasting in with a dead rudder. But there was a way of reversing them, if you learned the trick, by cutting the switch and putting it on again exactly on the final dying revolution of the flywheel, so that it would kick back against compression and begin re-

versing. Approaching a dock in a strong following breeze, it was difficult to slow up sufficiently by the ordinary coasting method, and if a boy felt he had complete mastery over his motor, he was tempted to keep it running beyond its time and then reverse it a few feet from the dock. It took a cool nerve, because if you threw the switch a twentieth of a second too soon you would catch the flywheel when it still had speed enough to go up past center, and the boat would leap ahead, charging bull-fashion at the dock.

We had a good week at the camp. The bass were biting well and the sun shone endlessly, day after day. We would be tired at night and lie down in the accumulated heat of the little bedrooms after the long hot day and the breeze would stir almost imperceptibly outside and the smell of the swamp drift in through the rusty screens. Sleep would come easily and in the morning the red squirrel would be on the roof, tapping out his gay routine. I kept remembering everything, lying in bed in the mornings—the small steamboat that had a long rounded stern like the lip of a Ubangi, and how quietly she ran on the moonlight sails, when the older boys played their mandolins and the girls sang and we ate doughnuts dipped in sugar, and how sweet the music was on the water in the shining night, and what it had felt like to think about girls then. After breakfast we would go up to the store and the things were in the same place—the minnows in a bottle, the plugs and spinners disarranged and pawed over by the youngsters from the boys' camp, the Fig Newtons and the Beeman's gum. Outside, the road was tarred and cars stood in front of the store. Inside, all was just as it had always been, except there was more Coca-Cola and not so much Moxie and root beer and birch beer and sarsaparilla. We would walk out with a bottle of pop apiece and sometimes the pop would backfire up our noses and hurt. We explored the streams, quietly, where the turtles slid off the sunny logs and dug their way into the soft bottom; and we lay on the town wharf and fed worms to the tame bass. Everywhere we went I had trouble making out which was I, the one walking at my side, the one walking in my pants.

One afternoon while we were there at that lake a thunderstorm came up. It was like the revival of an old melodrama that I had seen long ago with childish awe. The second-act climax of the drama of the electrical disturbance over a lake in America had not changed in any important respect. This was the big scene, still the big scene. The whole thing was so familiar, the first feeling of oppression and heat and a general air around camp of not wanting to go very far away. In midafternoon (it was all the same) a curious darkening of the sky, and a lull in everything that had made life tick; and then the way the boats suddenly swung the other way at their moorings with the coming of a breeze out of the new quarter, and the premonitory rumble. Then the kettle drum, then the snare, then the bass drum and cymbals, then crackling light against the dark, and the gods grinning and licking their chops in the hills. Afterward the calm, the rain steadily rustling in the calm lake, the return of light and hope and spirits, and the campers running out in joy and relief to go swimming in the rain, their bright cries perpetuating the deathless joke about how they were getting simply drenched, and the children screaming with delight at the new sensation of bathing in the rain, and the joke about getting drenched linking the generations in a strong indestructible chain. And the comedian who waded in carrying an umbrella.

When the others went swimming, my son said he was going in, too. He pulled his dripping trunks from the line where they had hung all through the shower, and wrung them out. Languidly, and with no thought of going in, I watched him, his hard little body, skinny and bare, saw him wince slightly as he pulled up around his vitals the small, soggy, icy garment. As he buckled the swollen belt, suddenly my groin felt the chill of death.

My Wood

E. M. Forster

*E. M. (Edward Morgan) Forster (1879–1970)—novelist,
essayist, biographer, and literary critic—was born in London and educated at Cambridge. A member of the Bloomsbury Group of writers and artists (so named for the
Bloomsbury residential district in central London), Forster
published a number of renowned works, including* Where
Angels Fear to Tread *(1905),* A Room with a View
1908), Howard's End *(1910), and what is considered to
be his masterpiece,* A Passage to India *(1924). He also
published several volumes of short stories and essays. In
1951, while in his 70s, Forster collaborated with Eric
Crozier on the libretto of the opera "Billy Budd." A recurring theme of Forster's work was the impact of society on
human relationships. In this essay (published in 1936 in*
Abinger Harvest, *an essay collection), Forster muses on the
profits and impositions of property ownership, noting the
deterioration of the moral fiber of the land owner. As you
read, think of the relevance of Forster's arguments today,
more than half a century after it was written.*

1   A few years ago I wrote a book which dealt in part with the difficulties of the English in India. Feeling that they would have
had no difficulties in India themselves, the Americans read the
book freely. The more they read it the better it made them feel, and a
cheque to the author was the result. I bought a wood with the cheque.
It is not a large wood—it contains scarcely any trees, and it is inter-
sected, blast it, by a public footpath. Still, it is the first property that
I have owned, so it is right that other people should participate in my
shame, and should ask themselves, in accents that will vary in horror,

this very important question: What is the effect of property upon the character? Don't let's touch economics; the effect of private ownership upon the community as a whole is another question—a more important question, perhaps, but another one. Let's keep to psychology. If you own things, what's their effect on you? What's the effect on me of my wood?

In the first place, it makes me feel heavy. Property does have this effect. Property produces men of weight, and it was a man of weight who failed to get into the Kingdom of Heaven. He was not wicked, that unfortunate millionaire in the parable, he was only stout; he stuck out in front, not to mention behind, and as he wedged himself this way and that in the crystalline entrance and bruised his well-fed flanks, he saw beneath him a comparatively slim camel passing through the eye of a needle and being woven into the robe of God. The Gospels all through couple stoutness and slowness. They point out what is perfectly obvious, yet seldom realized: that if you have a lot of things you cannot move about a lot, that furniture requires dusting, dusters require servants, servants require insurance stamps, and the whole tangle of them makes you think twice before you accept an invitation to dinner or go for a bathe in the Jordan. Sometimes the Gospels proceed further and say with Tolstoy that property is sinful; they approach the difficult ground of asceticism here, where I cannot follow them. But as to the immediate effects of property on people, they just show straightforward logic. It produces men of weight. Men of weight cannot, by definition, move like the lightning from the East unto the West, and the ascent of a fourteen-stone bishop into a pulpit is thus the exact antithesis of the coming of the Son of Man. My wood makes me feel heavy.

In the second place, it makes me feel it ought to be larger.

The other day I heard a twig snap in it. I was annoyed at first, for I thought that someone was blackberrying, and depreciating the value of the undergrowth. On coming nearer, I saw it was not a man who had trodden on the twig and snapped it, but a bird, and I felt pleased. My bird. The bird was not equally pleased. Ignoring the relation between us, it took flight as soon as it saw the shape of my face, and flew straight over the boundary hedge into a field, the property of Mrs. Henessy, where it sat down with a loud squawk. It had become Mrs. Henessy's bird. Something seemed grossly amiss here, something that would not have occurred had the wood been larger. I could not afford to buy Mrs. Henessy out, I dared not murder her, and limitations of this sort beset me on every side. Ahab did not want that vineyard—he only needed it to round off his property, preparatory to plotting a new curve—and all the land around my wood has become necessary to me in order to round off the wood. A boundary protects. But—poor little thing—the boundary ought in its turn to be protected. Noises on the edge of it. Children throw stones. A little more, and then a little more, until we reach the sea. Happy Canute! Happier Alexander! And after all, why should even the world be the limit of possession? A rocket containing a Union Jack, will, it is hoped, be shortly fired at the moon. Mars. Sirius. Beyond which . . . But these immensities ended by saddening me. I could not suppose that my wood was the destined nucleus of universal dominion—it is so very small and contains no mineral wealth beyond the blackberries. Nor was I comforted when Mrs. Henessy's bird took alarm for the second time and flew clean away from us all, under the belief that it belonged to itself.

5   In the third place, property makes its owner feel that he ought to do something to it. Yet he isn't sure what. A restlessness comes over him, a vague sense that he has a personality to express—the same sense which, without any vagueness, leads the artist to an act of creation. Sometimes I think I will cut down such trees as remain in the wood, at other times I want to fill up the gaps between them with new trees. Both impulses are pretentious and empty. They are not honest movements toward money-making or beauty. They spring from a foolish desire to express myself and from an inability to enjoy what I have got. Creation, property, enjoyment form a sinister trinity in the human mind. Creation and enjoyment are both very, very good, yet they are often unattainable without a material basis, and at such moments property pushes itself in as a substitute, saying, "Accept me instead—I'm good enough for all three." It is not enough. It is, as Shakespeare said of lust, "The expense of spirit in a waste of shame": it is "Before, a joy proposed; behind, a dream." Yet we don't know how to shun it. It is forced on us by our economic system as the alternative to starvation. It is also forced on us by an internal defect in the soul, by the feeling that in property may lie the germs of self-development and of exquisite or heroic deeds. Our life on earth is, and ought to be, material and carnal. But we have not yet learned to manage our materialism and carnality properly; they are still entangled with the desire for

ownership, where (in the words of Dante) "Possession is one with loss."

And this brings us to our fourth and final point: the blackberries.

Blackberries are not plentiful in this meagre grove, but they are easily seen from the public footpath which traverses it, and all too easily gathered. Foxgloves, too—people will pull up the foxgloves, and ladies of an educational tendency even grub for toadstools to show them on the Monday in class. Other ladies, less educated, roll down the bracken in the arms of their gentlemen friends. There is paper, there are tins. Pray does my wood belong to me or doesn't it? And, if it does, should I not own it best by allowing no one else to walk there? There is a wood near Lyme Regis, also cursed by a public footpath, where the owner has not hesitated on this point. He had built high stone walls each side of the path, and has spanned it by bridges, so that the public circulate like termites while he gorges on the blackberries unseen. He really does own his wood, this able chap. Dives in Hell did pretty well, but the gulf dividing him from Lazarus could be traversed by vision, and nothing traverses it here. And perhaps I shall come to this in time. I shall wall in and fence out until I really taste the sweets of property. Enormously stout, endlessly avaricious, pseudo-creative, intensely selfish, I shall weave upon my forehead the quadruple crown of possession until those nasty Bolshies come and take it off again and thrust me aside into the outer darkness.

Politics and the English Language

George Orwell

*George Orwell is the pen name used by the British author
Eric Blair (1903–1950). Orwell was born in the Indian
village of Motihari, near Nepal, where his father was sta-
tioned in the Civil Service. India was then part of the
British Empire. From 1907 to 1922 Orwell lived in England, returning to India and Burma and a position in the
Imperial Police, which he held until 1927. Thereafter he
lived in England, Paris, Spain, and elsewhere, writing on
a wide range of topics. He fought in the Spanish Civil War
and was actively engaged in several political movements,
always against totalitarianism of any kind. He is best
known today for two novels of political satire:* Animal
Farm *(1945) and* 1984 *(1949). He was also a prolific
journalist and essayist, with his essays collected in five volumes. He wrote "Politics and the English Language"
shortly after the end of World War II, at a time when patriotic fervor was very strong in the Allied countries such as
England the United States, while Marxist ideology was
growing elsewhere. Orwell was particularly sensitive to the
use of language for political purposes, which he saw as a
special instance of a more general corruption of the English
language. In the 50 years since this was written, many of
the phrases Orwell writes about have dropped from common use, so you may have difficulty understanding some of
his examples. Nonetheless, his general points will be quite
clear, and you will be able to find contemporary analogues
to his examples.*

Reprinted from *Shooting an Elephant and Other Essays* (1950), by permission of
Penguin Group Ltd., A.M. Heath and Harcourt Brace and Company.

1   **M**ost people who bother with the matter at all would admit   1
that the English language is in a bad way, but it is generally
assumed that we cannot by conscious action do anything
about it. Our civilization is decadent and our language—so the argument runs—must inevitably share in the general collapse. It follows
that any struggle against the abuse of language is a sentimental archaism, like preferring candles to electric light or hansom cabs to air-
planes. Underneath this lies the half-conscious belief that language is
a natural growth and not an instrument which we shape for our own
purposes.

Now, it is clear that the decline of a language must ultimately have
political and economic causes: it is not due simply to the bad influence of this or that individual writer. But an effect can become a cause,
reinforcing the original cause and producing the same effect in an in-
tensified form, and so on indefinitely. A man may take to drink because he feels himself to be a failure, and then fail all the more
completely because he drinks. It is rather the same thing that is happening to the English language. It becomes ugly and inaccurate because our thoughts are foolish, but the slovenliness of our language
makes it easier for us to have foolish thoughts. The point is that the
process is reversible. Modern English, especially written English, is full
of bad habits which spread by imitation and which can be avoided if
one is willing to take the necessary trouble. If one gets rid of these
habits one can think more clearly, and to think clearly is a necessary
first step towards political regeneration: so that the fight against bad
English is not frivolous and is not the exclusive concern of professional
writers. I will come back to this presently, and I hope that by that time
the meaning of what I have said here will have become clearer. Mean-
while, here are five specimens of the English language as it is now habitually written.

These five passages have not been picked out because they are especially bad—I could have quoted far worse if I had chosen—but because they illustrate various of the mental vices from which we now
suffer. They are a little below the average, but are fairly representative samples. I number them so that I can refer back to them when
necessary:

*"(1) I am not, indeed, sure whether it is not true to say that the
Milton who once seemed not unlike a seventeenth-century Shelley*

had not become, out of an experience ever more bitter in each year, more alien (sic) *to the founder of that Jesuit sect which nothing could induce him to tolerate."*

Professor Harold Laski (Essay in *Freedom of Expression*).

"(2) Above all, we cannot play ducks and drakes with a native battery of idioms which prescribes such egregious collocations of vocables as the Basic put up with *for* tolerate *or* put at a loss *for* bewilder."

Professor Lancelot Hogben (*Interglossa*).

"(3) On the one side we have the free personality: by definition it is not neurotic, for it has neither conflict nor dream. Its desires, such as they are, are transparent, for they are just what institutional approval keeps in the forefront of consciousness; another institutional pattern would alter their number and intensity; there is little in them that is natural, irreducible, or culturally dangerous. But on the other side, the social bond itself is nothing but the mutual reflection of these self-secure integrities. Recall the definition of love. Is not this the very picture of a small academic? Where is there a place in this hall of mirrors for either personality or fraternity?"

Essay on psychology in *Politics* (New York).

"(4) All the 'best people' from the gentlemen's clubs, and all the frantic fascist captains, united in common hatred of Socialism and bestial horror of the rising tide of the mass revolutionary movement, have turned to acts of provocation, to foul incendiarism, to medieval legends of poisoned wells, to legalize their own destruction of proletarian organizations, and rouse the agitated petty-bourgeoisie to chauvinistic fervor on behalf of the fight against the revolutionary way out of the crisis."

Communist pamphlet.

"(5) If a new spirit is to be infused into this old country, there is one thorny and contentious reform which must be tackled, and that is the humanization and galvanization of the B.B.C. Timidity here will bespeak cancer and atrophy of the soul. The heart of Britain may be sound and of strong beat, for instance, but the British lion's roar at present is like that of Bottom in Shakespeare's Midsummer Night's Dream—*as gentle as any sucking dove. A virile new*

Britain cannot continue indefinitely to be traduced in the eyes or rather ears, of the world by the effete languors of Langham Place, brazenly masquerading as 'standard English'. When the Voice of Britain is heard at nine o'clock, better far and infinitely less ludicrous to hear aitches honestly dropped than the present priggish, inflated, inhibited, school-ma'amish arch braying of blameless bashful mewing maidens!"

Letter in *Tribune.*

Each of these passages has faults of its own, but, quite apart from avoidable ugliness, two qualities are common to all of them. The first is staleness of imagery: the other is lack of precision. The writer either has a meaning and cannot express it, or he inadvertently says something else, or he is almost indifferent as to whether his words mean anything or not. This mixture of vagueness and sheer incompetence is the most marked characteristic of modern English prose, and especially of any kind of political writing. As soon as certain topics are raised, the concrete melts into the abstract and no one seems able to think of turns of speech that are not hackneyed: prose consists less and less of words chosen for the sake of their meaning, and more and more of phrases tacked together like the sections of a prefabricated henhouse. I list below, with notes and examples, various of the tricks by means of which the work of prose-construction is habitually dodged:

Dying Metaphors

5   A newly invented metaphor assists thought by evoking a visual image,   5
while on the other hand a metaphor which is technically "dead" (e.g. *iron resolution*) has in effect reverted to being an ordinary word and can generally be used without loss of vividness. But in between these two classes there is a huge dump of worn-out metaphors which have lost all evocative power and are merely used because they save people the trouble of inventing phrases for themselves. Examples are: *Ring the changes on, take up the cudgels for, toe the line, ride roughshod over, stand shoulder to shoulder with, play into the hands of, no axe to grind, grist to the mill, fishing in troubled waters, on the order of the day, Achilles' heel, swan song, hotbed.* Many of these are used without knowledge of their meaning (what is a "rift," for instance?), and incompatible metaphors are frequently mixed, a sure sign that the writer is not interested in

what he is saying. Some metaphors now current have been twisted out of their original meaning without those who use them even being aware of the fact. For example, *toe the line* is sometimes written *tow the line*. Another example is *the hammer and the anvil,* now always used with the implication that the anvil gets the worst of it. In real life it is always the anvil that breaks the hammer, never the other way about: a writer who stopped to think what he was saying would be aware of this, and would avoid perverting the original phrase.

Operators or Verbal False Limbs

These save the trouble of picking out appropriate verbs and nouns, and at the same time pad each sentence with extra syllables which give it an appearance of symmetry. Characteristic phrases are: *render inoperative, militate against, make contact with, be subjected to, give rise to, give grounds for, have the effect of, play a leading part (role) in, make itself felt, take effect, exhibit a tendency to, serve the purpose of, etc., etc.* The keynote is the elimination of simple verbs. Instead of being a single word, such as *break, stop, spoil, mend, kill,* a verb becomes a *phrase,* made up of a noun or adjective tacked on to some general-purposes verb such as *prove, serve, form, play, render.* In addition, the passive voice is wherever possible used in preference to the active, and noun constructions are used instead of gerunds (*by examination of* instead of *by examining*). The range of verbs is further cut down by means of the *-ize* and *de-* formation, and the banal statements are given an appearance of profundity by means of the *not un-* formation. Simple conjunctions and prepositions are replaced by such phrases as *with respect to, having regard to, the fact that, by dint of, in view of, in the interests of, on the hypothesis that;* and the ends of sentences are saved from anticlimax by such resounding commonplaces as *greatly to be desired, cannot be left out of account, a development to be expected in the near future, deserving of serious consideration, brought to a satisfactory conclusion,* and so on and so forth.

Pretentious Diction

Words like *phenomenon, element, individual* (as noun), *objective, categorical, effective, virtual, basic, primary, promote, constitute, inhibit, exploit, utilize, eliminate, liquidate,* are used to dress up simple statements and give an air of scientific impartiality to biased judgments.

Adjectives like *epoch-making, epic, historic, unforgettable, triumphant, age-old, inevitable, inexorable, veritable,* are used to dignify the sordid processes of international politics, while writing that aims at glorifying war usually takes on an archaic color, its characteristic words being: *realm, throne, chariot, mailed fist, trident, sword, shield, buckler, banner, jackboot, clarion.* Foreign words and expressions such as *cul de sac, ancien régime, deus ex machina, mutatis mutandis, status quo, gleichschaltung, weltanschauung,* are used to give an air of culture and elegance. Except for the useful abbreviations *i.e., e.g.,* and *etc.,* there is no real need for any of the hundreds of foreign phrases now current in English. Bad writers, and especially scientific, political and sociological writers, are nearly always haunted by the notion that Latin or Greek words are grander than Saxon ones, and unnecessary words like *expedite, ameliorate, predict, extraneous, deracinated, clandestine, subaqueous* and hundreds of others constantly gain ground from their Anglo-Saxon opposite numbers. The jargon peculiar to Marxist writing (*hyena, hangman, cannibal, petty bourgeois, these, gentry, lacquey, flunkey, mad dog, White Guard,* etc.) consists largely of words and phrases translated from Russian, German or French; but the normal way of coining a new word is to use a Latin or Greek root with the appropriate affix and, where necessary, the *-ize* formation. It is often easier to make up words of this kind (*deregionalize, impermissible, extramarital, non-fragmentory* and so forth) than to think up the English words that will cover one's meaning. The result, in general, is an increase in slovenliness and vagueness.

Meaningless Words

In certain kinds of writing, particularly in art criticism and literary criticism, it is normal to come across long passages which are almost completely lacking in meaning. Words like *romantic, plastic, values, human, dead, sentimental, natural, vitality,* as used in art criticism, are strictly meaningless in the sense that they not only do not point to any discoverable object, but are hardly ever expected to do so by the reader. When one critic writes, "The outstanding feature of Mr. X's work is its living quality", while another writes, "The immediately striking thing about Mr. X's work is its peculiar deadness", the reader accepts this as a simple difference of opinion. If words like *black* and *white* were involved, instead of the jargon words *dead* and *living,* he would see at once that language was being used in an improper way. Many political words are similarly abused. The word *Fascism* has now no meaning except in so far as it signifies "something not desirable." The words *democracy, socialism, freedom, patriotic, realistic, justice,* have each of them several different meanings which cannot be reconciled with one another. In the case of a word like *democracy,* not only is there no agreed definition, but the attempt to make one is resisted from all sides. It is almost universally felt that when we call a country democratic we are praising it: consequently the defenders of every kind of régime claim that it is a democracy, and fear that they might have to stop using the word if it were tied down to any one meaning. Words of this kind are often used in a consciously dishonest way. That is, the person who uses them has his own private definition, but allows his hearer to think he means something quite different. Statements like *Marshal Pétain was a true patriot, The Soviet Press is the freest in the world, The Catholic Church is opposed to persecution,* are almost always made with intent to deceive. Other words used in variable meanings, in most cases more or less dishonestly, are: *class, totalitarian, science, progressive, reactionary, bourgeois, equality.*

Now that I have made this catalogue of swindles and perversions, let me give another example of the kind of writing that they lead to. This time it must of its nature be an imaginary one. I am going to translate a passage of good English into modern English of the worst sort. Here is a well-known verse from *Ecclesiastes:*

> *"I returned and saw under the sun, that the race is not to the swift, nor the battle to the strong, neither yet bread to the wise, nor yet riches to men of understanding, nor yet favour to men of skill; but time and chance happeneth to them all."*

Here it is in modern English:

> *"Objective consideration of contemporary phenomena compels the conclusion that success or failure in competitive activities exhibits no tendency to be commensurate with innate capacity, but that a considerable element of the unpredictable must invariably be taken into account."*

This is a parody, but not a very gross one. Exhibit (3), above, for instance, contains several patches of the same kind of English. It will be seen that I have not made a full translation. The beginning and ending of the sentence follow the original meaning fairly closely, but in the middle the concrete illustrations—race, battle, bread—dissolve into the vague phrase "success or failure in competitive activities." This had to be so, because no modern writer of the kind I am discussing—no one capable of using phrases like "objective consideration of contemporary phenomena"—would ever tabulate his thoughts in that precise and detailed way. The whole tendency of modern prose is away from concreteness. Now analyze these two sentences a little more closely. The first contains forty-nine words but only sixty syllables, and all its words are those of everyday life. The second contains thirty-eight words of ninety syllables: eighteen of its words are from Latin roots, and one from Greek. The first sentence contains six vivid images, and only one phrase ("time and chance") that could be called vague. The second contains not a single fresh, arresting phrase, and in spite of its ninety syllables it gives only a shortened version of the meaning contained in the first. Yet without a doubt it is the second kind of sentence that is gaining ground in modern English. I do not want to exaggerate. This kind of writing is not yet universal, and outcrops of simplicity will occur here and there in the worst-written page. Still, if you or I were told to write a few lines on the uncertainty of human fortunes, we should probably come much nearer to my imaginary sentence than to the one from *Ecclesiastes*.

As I have tried to show, modern writing at its worst does not consist in picking out words for the sake of their meaning and inventing images in order to make the meaning clearer. It consists in gumming together long strips of words which have already been set in order by someone else, and making the results presentable by sheer humbug. The attraction of this way of writing is that it is easy. It is easier—even quicker, once you have the habit—to say *In my opinion it is a not unjustifiable assumption* that than to say *I think*. If you use ready-made phrases, you not only don't have to hunt about for words; you also don't have to bother with the rhythms of your sentences, since these phrases are generally so arranged as to be more or less euphonious. When you are composing in a hurry—when you are dictating to a stenographer, for instance, or making a public speech—it is natural to fall into a pretentious, Latinized style. Tags like *a consideration which we should do well to bear in mind* or *a conclusion to which all of us would readily assent* will save many a sentence from coming down with a bump. By using stale metaphors, similes and idioms, you save much mental effort, at the cost of leaving your meaning vague, not only for your reader but for yourself. This is the significance of mixed metaphors. The sole aim of a metaphor is to call up a visual image. When these images clash—as in *The Fascist octopus has sung its swan song, the jackboot is thrown into the melting pot*—it can't be taken as certain that the writer is not seeing a mental image of the objects he is naming; in other words he is not really thinking. Look again at the examples I gave at the beginning of this essay. Professor Laski (1) uses five negatives in fifty-three words. One of these is superfluous, making nonsense of the whole passage, and in addition there is the slip *alien* for akin, making further nonsense, and several avoidable pieces of clumsiness which increase the general vagueness. Professor Hogben (2) plays ducks and drakes with a battery which is able to write prescriptions, and, while disapproving of the everyday phrase *put up with,* is unwilling to look *egregious* up in the dictionary and see what it means. (3), if one takes an uncharitable attitude towards it, is simply meaningless: probably one could work out its intended meaning by reading the whole of the article in which it occurs. In (4), the writer knows more or less what he wants to say, but an accumulation of stale phrases chokes him like tea leaves blocking a sink. In (5), words and meaning have almost parted company. People who write in this manner usually have a general emotional meaning—they dislike one thing and want to express solidarity with another—but they are not interested in the detail of what they are saying. A scrupulous writer, in every sentence that he writes, will ask himself at least four questions, thus: What am I trying to say? What words will express it? What image or idiom will make it clearer? Is this image fresh enough to have an effect? And he will probably ask himself two more: Could I put it more shortly? Have I said anything that is avoidably ugly? But you are not obliged to go to all this trouble. You can shirk it by simply throwing your mind open and letting the ready-made phrases come crowding in. They will construct your sentences for you—even think your thoughts for you, to a certain extent—and at need they will perform the important service of partially concealing your meaning even from yourself. It is at this point that the special connection between politics and the debasement of language becomes clear.

In our time it is broadly true that political writing is bad writing. Where it is not true, it will generally be found that the writer is some kind of rebel, expressing his private opinions and not a "party line."

Orthodoxy, of whatever colour, seems to demand a lifeless, imitative style. The political dialects to be found in pamphlets, leading articles, manifestos, White Papers and the speeches of under-secretaries do, of course, vary from party to party, but they are all alike in that one almost never finds in them a fresh, vivid, home-made turn of speech. When one watches some tired hack on the platform mechanically repeating the familiar phrases—*bestial atrocities, iron heel, bloodstained tyranny, free peoples of the world, stand shoulder to shoulder*—one often has a curious feeling that one is not watching a live human being but some kind of dummy: a feeling which suddenly becomes stronger at moments when the light catches the speaker's spectacles and turns them into blank discs which seem to have no eyes behind them. And this is not altogether fanciful. A speaker who uses that kind of phraseology has gone some distance towards turning himself into a machine. The appropriate noises are coming out of his larynx, but his brain is not involved as it would be if he were choosing his words for himself. If the speech he is making is one that he is accustomed to make over and over again, he may be almost unconscious of what he is saying, as one is when one utters the responses in church. And this reduced state of consciousness, if not indispensable, is at any rate favorable to political conformity.

In our time, political speech and writing are largely the defence of the indefensible. Things like the continuance of British rule in India, the Russian purges and deportations, the dropping of the atom bombs on Japan, can indeed be defended, but only by arguments which are too brutal for most people to face, and which do not square with the professed aims of political parties. Thus political language has to consist largely of euphemism, question-begging and sheer cloudy vagueness. Defenceless villages are bombarded from the air, the inhabitants driven out into the countryside, the cattle machine-gunned, the huts set on fire with incendiary bullets: this is called *pacification*. Millions of peasants are robbed of their farms and sent trudging along the roads with no more than they can carry: this is called *transfer of population* or *rectification of frontiers*. People are imprisoned for years without trial, or shot in the back of the neck or sent to die of scurvy in Arctic lumber camps: this is called *elimination of unreliable elements*. Such phraseology is needed if one wants to name things without calling up mental pictures of them. Consider for instance some comfortable English professor defending Russian totalitarianism. He cannot say outright, "I believe in killing off your opponents when you can get good results by doing so." Probably, therefore, he will say something like this:

15   "While freely conceding that the Soviet régime exhibits certain   15 features which the humanitarian may be inclined to deplore, we must, I think, agree that a certain curtailment of the right to political opposition is an unavoidable concomitant of transitional periods, and that the rigors which the Russian people have been called upon to undergo have been amply justified in the sphere of concrete achievement."

The inflated style is itself a kind of euphemism. A mass of Latin words falls upon the facts like soft snow, blurring the outlines and covering up all the details. The great enemy of clear language is insincerity. When there is a gap between one's real and one's declared aims, one turns as it were instinctively to long words and exhausted idioms, like a cuttlefish squirting out ink. In our age there is no such thing as "keeping out of politics." All issues are political issues, and politics itself is a mass of lies, evasions, folly, hatred and schizophrenia. When the general atmosphere is bad, language must suffer. I should expect to find—this is a guess which I have not sufficient knowledge to verify—that the German, Russian and Italian languages have all deteriorated in the last ten to fifteen years, as a result of dictatorship.

But if thought corrupts language, language can also corrupt thought. A bad usage can spread by tradition and imitation, even among people who should and do know better. The debased language that I have been discussing is in some ways very convenient. Phrases like *a not unjustifiable assumption, leaves much to be desired, would serve no good purpose, a consideration which we should do well to bear in mind,* are a continuous temptation, a packet of aspirins always at one's elbow. Look back through this essay, and for certain you will find that I have again and again committed the very faults I am protesting against. By this morning's post I have received a pamphlet dealing with conditions in Germany. The author tells me that he "felt impelled" to write it. I open it at random, and here is almost the first sentence that I see: "(The Allies) have an opportunity not only of achieving a radical transformation of Germany's social and political structure in such a way as to avoid a nationalistic reaction in Germany itself, but at the same time of laying the foundations of a cooperative and unified Europe." You see, he "feels impelled" to write—feels, presumably, that he has something new to say—and yet his words, like cavalry horses answering the bugle, group themselves automatically into the familiar dreary pattern. This invasion of one's mind by ready-made phrases (*lay the foundations, achieve a radical transformation*) can only be prevented if one is constantly on guard against them, and every such phrase anaesthetizes a portion of one's brain.

I said earlier that the decadence of our language is probably curable. Those who deny this would argue, if they produced an argument at all, that language merely reflects existing social conditions, and that we cannot influence its development by any direct tinkering with words and constructions. So far as the general tone or spirit of a language goes, this may be true, but it is not true in detail. Silly words and expressions have often disappeared, not through any evolutionary process but owing to the conscious action of a minority. Two recent examples were *explore every avenue* and *leave no stone unturned,* which were killed by the jeers of a few journalists. There is a long list of fly-blown metaphors which could similarly be got rid of if enough people would interest themselves in the job; and it should also be possible to laugh the *not un-* formation out of existence, to reduce the amount of Latin and Greek in the average sentence, to drive out foreign phrases and strayed scientific words, and, in general, to make pretentiousness unfashionable. But all these are minor points. The defence of the English language implies more than this, and perhaps it is best to start by saying what it does not imply.

To begin with it has nothing to do with archaism, with the salvaging of obsolete words and turns of speech, or with the setting up of a "standard English" which must never be departed from. On the contrary, it is especially concerned with the scrapping of every word or idiom which has outworn its usefulness. It has nothing to do with correct grammar and syntax, which are of no importance so long as one makes one's meaning clear, or with the avoidance of Americanisms, or with having what is called a "good prose style." On the other hand it is not concerned with fake simplicity and the attempt to make written English colloquial. Nor does it even imply in every case preferring the Saxon word to the Latin one, though it does imply using the fewest and shortest words that will cover one's meaning. What is above all needed is to let the meaning choose the word, and not the other way about. In prose, the worst thing one can do with words is to surrender to them. When you think of a concrete object, you think wordlessly, and then, if you want to describe the thing you have been visualizing you probably hunt about till you find the exact words that seem to fit. When you think of something abstract you are more inclined to use words from the start, and unless you make a conscious effort to prevent it, the existing dialect will come rushing in and do the job for you, at the expense of blurring or even changing your meaning. Probably it is better to put off using words as long as possible and get one's meaning as clear as one can through pictures or sensations. Afterwards one can choose—not simply accept—the phrases that will best cover the meaning, and then switch round and decide what impression one's words are likely to make on another person. This last effort of the mind cuts out all stale or mixed images, all prefabricated phrases, needless repetitions, and humbug and vagueness generally. But one can often be in doubt about the effect of a word or a phrase, and one needs rules that one can rely on when instinct fails. I think the following rules will cover most cases:

(i) Never use a metaphor, simile or other figure of speech which you are used to seeing in print.

(ii) Never use a long word where a short one will do.

(iii) If it is possible to cut a word out, always cut it out.

(iv) Never use the passive where you can use the active.

(v) Never use a foreign phrase, a scientific word or a jargon word if you can think of an everyday English equivalent.

(vi) Break any of these rules sooner than say anything outright barbarous.

20   These rules sound elementary, and so they are, but they demand   20
a deep change of attitude in anyone who has grown used to writing in the style now fashionable. One could keep all of them and still write bad English, but one could not write the kind of stuff that I quoted in those five specimens at the beginning of this article.

I have not here been considering the literary use of language, but merely language as an instrument for expressing and not for concealing or preventing thought. Stuart Chase and others have come near to claiming that all abstract words are meaningless, and have used this as a pretext for advocating a kind of political quietism. Since you don't know what Fascism is, how can you struggle against Fascism? One need not swallow such absurdities as this, but one ought to recognize that the present political chaos is connected with the decay of language, and that one can probably bring about some improvement by starting at the verbal end. If you simplify your English, you are freed from the worst follies of orthodoxy. You cannot speak any of the necessary dialects, and when you make a stupid remark its stupidity will be obvious, even to yourself. Political language—and with variations this is true of all political parties, from Conservatives to Anarchists—is designed to make lies sound truthful and murder respectable, and to give an appearance of solidity to pure wind. One cannot change this all in a moment, but one can at least change one's own habits, and from time to time one can even, if one jeers loudly enough, send some worn-out and useless phrase—some *jackboot, Achilles' heel, hotbed, melting pot, acid test, veritable inferno* or other lump of verbal refuse—into the dustbin where it belongs.

"I'm Not Racist But . . ."

Neil Bissoondath

Born in Trinidad, Neil Bissoondath (1955–) moved to Canada at age 18 to attend York University. Upon receiving a degree in French, Bissoondath taught both French and English before beginning his writing career. In choosing to be a full-time writer, he followed in the footsteps of his internationally known uncles, Shiva and V.S. Naipaul. Bissoondath's first book, the short story collection Digging Up the Mountains *(1985), received significant critical praise, and his nonfiction critique of multiculturalism,* Selling Illusions: The Cult of Multiculturalism in Canada *(1994), stirred a good deal of controversy. His book* The Innocence of Age *(1992) won the Canadian Authors Association Prize for fiction. Most of Bissoondath's work, both fiction and nonfiction, deals with the dislocation, alienation, and racial tension of non-white immigrants in Canadian society. In the following essay, the author questions the legitimacy of labeling all insensitive ethnic language as racism.*

1   Someone recently said that racism is as Canadian as maple syrup. I have no argument with that. History provides us with ample proof. But, for proper perspective, let us remember that it is also as American as apple pie, as French as croissants, as Jamaican as ackee, as Indian as aloo, as Chinese as chow mein, as. . . . Well, there's an entire menu to be written. This is not by way of excusing it. Murder and rape, too, are international, multicultural, as innate to the darker side of the human experience. But we must be careful that the inevitable rage evoked does not blind us to the larger context.

     The word "racism" is a discomforting one: It is so vulnerable to manipulation. We can, if we so wish, apply it to any incident involving people of different colour. And therein lies the danger. During the heat of altercation, we seize, as terms of abuse, on whatever is most obvious about the person. It is, often, a question of unfortunate convenience. A woman, because of her sex, easily becomes a female dog or an intimate part of her anatomy. A large person might be dubbed "a stupid ox," a small person "a little" whatever. And so a black might become "a nigger," a white "a honky," an Asian "a paki," a Chinese "a chink," an Italian "a wop," a French-Canadian "a frog."

There is nothing pleasant about these terms; they assault every decent sensibility. Even so, I once met someone who, in a stunning surge of naiveté, used them as simple descriptives and not as terms of racial abuse. She was horrified to learn the truth. While this may have been an extreme case, the point is that the use of such patently abusive words may not always indicate racial or cultural distaste. They may indicate ignorance or stupidity or insensitivity, but pure racial hatred—such as the Nazis held for Jews, or the Ku Klux Klan for blacks—is a thankfully rare commodity.

Ignorance, not the willful kind but that which comes from lack of experience, is often indicated by that wonderful phrase, "I'm not racist but. . . ." I think of the mover, a friendly man, who said, "I'm not racist, but the Chinese are the worst drivers on the road." He was convinced this was so because the shape of their eyes, as far as he could surmise, denied them peripheral vision.

5 Or the oil company executive, an equally warm and friendly man, who, looking for an apartment in Toronto, rejected buildings with East Indian tenants not because of their race—he was telling me this, after all—but because he was given to understand that cockroaches were symbols of good luck in their culture and that, when they moved into a new home, friends came by with gift-wrapped cockroaches.

Neither of these men thought of himself as racist, and I believe they were not, deep down. (The oil company executive made it clear he would not hesitate to have me as a neighbour; my East Indian descent was of no consequence to him, my horror of cockroaches was.) Yet their comments, so innocently delivered, would open them to the accusation, justifiably so if this were all one knew about them. But it is a charge which would undoubtedly be wounding to them. It is difficult to recognize one's own misconceptions.

True racism is based, more often than not, on willful ignorance, and an acceptance of—and comfort with—stereotype. We like to think, in this country, that our multicultural mosaic will help nudge us into

84

a greater openness. But multiculturalism as we know it indulges in stereotype, depends on it for a dash of colour and the flash of dance. It fails to address the most basic questions people have about each other. Do those men doing the Dragon Dance really all belong to secret criminal societies? Do those women dressed in saris really coddle cockroaches for luck? Do those people in dreadlocks all smoke marijuana and live on welfare? Such questions do not seem to be the concern of the government's multicultural programs, superficial and exhibitionistic as they have become.

So the struggle against stereotype, the basis of all racism, becomes a purely personal one. We must beware of the impressions we create. A friend of mine once commented that, from talking to West Indians, she has the impression that their one great cultural contribution to the world is in the oft-repeated boast that "We (unlike everyone else) know how to party."

There are dangers, too, in community response. We must be wary of the self-appointed activists who seem to pop up in the media at every given opportunity spouting the rhetoric of retribution, mining distress for personal, political and professional gain. We must be skeptical about those who depend on conflict for their sense of self, the non-whites who need to feel themselves victims of racism, the whites who need to feel themselves purveyors of it. And we must be sure that, in addressing the problem, we do not end up creating it. Does the *Miss Black Canada Beauty Contest* still exist? I hope not. Not only do I find beauty contests offensive, but a racially segregated one even more so. What would the public reaction be, I wonder, if every year CTV broadcast the *Miss White Canada Beauty Pageant?* We give community-service awards only to blacks: Would we be comfortable with such awards only for whites? In Quebec, there are The Association of Black Nurses, The Association of Black Artists, The Congress of Black Jurists. Play tit for tat: The Association of White Nurses, White Artists, White Jurists: visions of apartheid. Let us be frank, racism for one is racism for others.

10   Finally, and perhaps most important, let us beware of abusing the   10 word itself.

Why We Crave Horror Movies
Stephen King

Stephen King (1947 –) was born in Portland, Maine. After graduating from the University of Maine in 1970, King held a number of jobs—knitting mill worker, janitor, high school English teacher—before gaining fame and fortune as a mystery writer. A prolific and widely popular writer (his book sales have surpassed 20 million copies), King has become synonymous with horror stories and movies. His many books include Carrie *(1974),* Salem's Lot *(1975),* The Shining *(1977),* The Dead Zone *(1979),* Firestarter *(1980),* Christine *(1983),* Pet Sematery *(1983),* Tommyknockers *(1984),* Misery *(1987),* Needful Things *(1991),* Insomnia *(1994),* Bag of Bones *(1998),* The Green Mile *(2000),* The Plant *(2000)—a serial novel which he published online,* The Colorado Kid *(2005), and* Cell *(2006). First published in* Playboy *in 1982, this essay explains, in the master's words, why we crave good horror shows.*

1   I think that we're all mentally ill; those of us outside the asylums only hide it a little better—and maybe not all that much better, after all. We've all known people who talk to themselves, people who sometimes squinch their faces into horrible grimaces when they believe no one is watching, people who have some hysterical fear—of snakes, the dark, the tight place, the long drop . . . and, of course, those final worms and grubs that are waiting so patiently underground.

When we pay our four or five bucks and seat ourselves at tenth-row center in a theater showing a horror movie, we are daring the nightmare.

Why? Some of the reasons are simple and obvious. To show that we can, that we are not afraid, that we can ride this roller coaster. Which is not to say that a really good horror movie may not surprise a scream out of us at some point, the way we may scream when the roller coaster twists through a complete 360 or plows through a lake at the bottom of the drop. And horror movies, like roller coasters, have always been the special province of the young; by the time one turns 40 or 50, one's appetite for double twists or 360-degree loops may be considerably depleted.

We also go to re-establish our feelings of essential normality; the horror movie is innately conservative, even reactionary. Freda Jackson as the horrible melting woman in *Die, Monster, Die!* confirms for us that no matter how far we may be removed from the beauty of a Robert Redford or a Diana Ross, we are still light-years from true ugliness.

5   And we go to have fun.   5

Ah, but this is where the ground starts to slope away, isn't it? Because this is a very peculiar sort of fun indeed. The fun comes from seeing others menaced—sometimes killed. One critic has suggested that if pro football has become the voyeur's version of combat, then the horror film has become the modern version of the public lynching.

It is true that the mythic, "fairytale" horror film intends to take away the shades of gray. . . . It urges us to put away our more civilized and adult penchant for analysis and to become children again, seeing things in pure blacks and whites. It may be that horror movies provide psychic relief on this level because this invitation to lapse into simplicity, irrationality and even outright madness is extended so rarely. We are told we may allow our emotions a free rein . . . or no rein at all.

If we are all insane, then sanity becomes a matter of degree. If your insanity leads you to carve up women like Jack the Ripper or the Cleveland Torso Murderer, we clap you away in the funny farm (but neither of those two amateur-night surgeons was ever caught, heh-heh-heh); if, on the other hand your insanity leads you only to talk to yourself when you're under stress or to pick your nose on your morning bus, then you are left alone to go about your business . . . though it is doubtful that you will ever be invited to the best parties.

The potential lyncher is in almost all of us (excluding saints, past and present; but then, most saints have been crazy in their own ways), and every now and then, he has to be let loose to scream and roll around in the grass. Our emotions and our fears form their own body, and we recognize that it demands its own exercise to maintain proper muscle tone.

Certain of these emotional muscles are accepted—even exalted—in civilized society; they are, of course, the emotions that tend to maintain the status quo of civilization itself. Love, friendship, loyalty, kindness—these are all the emotions that we applaud, emotions that have been immortalized in the couplets of Hallmark cards and in the verses (I don't dare call it poetry) of Leonard Nimoy.

10   When we exhibit these emotions, society showers us with positive reinforcement; we learn this even before we get out of diapers. When, as children, we hug our rotten little puke of a sister and give her a kiss, all the aunts and uncles smile and twit and cry, "Isn't he the sweetest little thing?" Such coveted treats as chocolate-covered graham crackers often follow. But if we deliberately slam the rotten little puke of a sister's fingers in the door, sanctions follow—angry remonstrance from parents, aunts and uncles; instead of a chocolate-covered graham cracker, a spanking.   10

But anticivilization emotions don't go away, and they demand periodic exercise. We have such "sick" jokes as, "What's the difference between a truckload of bowling balls and a truckload of dead babies?" (You can't unload a truckload of bowling balls with a pitchfork . . . a joke, by the way, that I heard originally from a ten-year-old.) Such a joke may surprise a laugh or a grin out of us even as we recoil, a possibility that confirms the thesis: If we share a brotherhood of man, then we also share an insanity of man. None of which is intended as a defense of either the sick joke or insanity but merely as an explanation of why the best horror films, like the best fairy tales, manage to be reactionary, anarchistic, and revolutionary all at the same time.

The mythic horror movie, like the sick joke, has a dirty job to do. It deliberately appeals to all that is worst in us. It is morbidity unchained, our most base instincts let free, our nastiest fantasies realized . . . and it all happens, fittingly enough, in the dark. For those reasons, good liberals often shy away from horror films. For myself, I like to see the most aggressive of them—*Dawn of the Dead,* for instance—as lifting a trap door in the civilized forebrain and throwing a basket of raw meat to the hungry alligators swimming around in that subterranean river beneath.

Why bother? Because it keeps them from getting out, man. It keeps them down there and me up here. It was Lennon and McCartney who said that all you need is love, and I would agree with that.

As long as you keep the gators fed.

The Female Body

Margaret Atwood

Margaret Atwood (1939–), born in Ottawa, Canada, at-
tended the University of Toronto, Radcliffe, and Harvard.
At a young age she decided to become a writer, and she has
published a remarkable list of novels, poetry, and essays,
along with forays into other genres such as children's stories
and television scripts. She is best known, however, for her
novels: The Edible Woman *(1969),* Surfacing *(1972),*
Lady Oracle *(1976),* Life Before Man *(1979),* Bodily
Harm *(1982),* The Handmaid's Tale *(1985),* Cat's Eye
(1989), The Robber Bride *(1994),* Alias Grace *(1996),*
The Blind Assassin *(2000),* Oryx and Crake *(2003),*
which was shortlisted for the Giller Prize, and the Man
Booker Prize, The Penelopiad *(2005), and* The Tent
(2006). In the following selection, published in 1992, she
uses an innovative approach to explore images of the female
body in our culture.

. . . entirely devoted to the subject of "The Female Body." Knowing
how well you have written on this topic . . . this capacious topic . . .

letter from Michigan Quarterly Review

1

1   I agree, it's a hot topic. But only one? Look around, there's a wide
range. Take my own, for instance.

I get up in the morning. My topic feels like hell. I sprinkle it with
water, brush parts of it, rub it with towels, powder it, add lubricant. I
dump in the fuel and away goes my topic, my topical topic, my controversial topic, my capacious topic, my limping topic, my nearsighted

topic, my topic with back problems, my badly behaved topic, my vulgar topic, my outrageous topic, my aging topic, my topic that is out of the question and anyway still can't spell, in its oversized coat and worn winter boots, scuttling along the sidewalk as if it were flesh and blood, hunting for what's out there, an avocado, an alderman, an adjective, hungry as ever.

2

The basic Female Body comes with the following accessories: garter belt, panti-girdle, crinoline, camisole, bustle, brassiere, stomacher, chemise, virgin zone, spike heels, nose ring, veil, kid gloves, fishnet stockings, fichu, bandeau, Merry Widow, weepers, chokers, barrettes, bangles, beads, lorgnette, feather boa, basic black, compact, Lycra stretch one-piece with modesty panel, designer peignoir, flannel nightie, lace teddy, bed, head.

3

The Female Body is made of transparent plastic and lights up when you plug it in. You press a button to illuminate the different systems. The circulatory system is red, for the heart and arteries, purple for the veins; the respiratory system is blue; the lymphatic system is yellow; the digestive system is green, with liver and kidneys in aqua. The nerves are done in orange and the brain is pink. The skeleton, as you might expect, is white.

5   The reproductive system is optional, and can be removed. It   5 comes with or without a miniature embryo. Parental judgment can thereby be exercised. We do not wish to frighten or offend.

4

He said, I won't have one of those things in the house. It gives a young girl a false notion of beauty, not to mention anatomy. If a real woman was built like that she'd fall on her face.

She said, If we don't let her have one like all the other girls she'll feel singled out. It'll become an issue. She'll long for one and she'll long to turn into one. Repression breeds sublimation. You know that.

He said, It's not just the pointy plastic tits, it's the wardrobes. The wardrobes and that stupid male doll, what's his name, the one with the underwear glued on.

She said, Better to get it over with when she's young. He said, All right, but don't let me see it.

10   She came whizzing down the stairs, thrown like a dart. She was   10 stark naked. Her hair had been chopped off, her head was turned back to front, she was missing some toes and she'd been tattooed all over her body with purple ink in a scrollwork design. She hit the potted azalea, trembled there for a moment like a botched angel, and fell.

He said, I guess we're safe.

5

The Female Body has many uses. It's been used as a door knocker, a bottle opener, as a clock with a ticking belly, as something to hold up lampshades, as a nutcracker, just squeeze the brass legs together and out comes your nut. It bears torches, lifts victorious wreaths, grows copper wings and raises aloft a ring of neon stars; whole buildings rest on its marble heads.

It sells cars, beer, shaving lotion, cigarettes, hard liquor; it sells diet plans and diamonds, and desire in tiny crystal bottles. Is this the face that launched a thousand products? You bet it is, but don't get any funny big ideas, honey, that smile is a dime a dozen.

It does not merely sell, it is sold. Money flows into this country or that country, flies in, practically crawls in, suitful after suitful, lured by all those hairless pre-teen legs. Listen, you want to reduce the national debt, don't you? Aren't you patriotic? That's the spirit. That's my girl.

15   She's a natural resource, a renewable one luckily, because those   15 things wear out so quickly. They don't make 'em like they used to. Shoddy goods.

6

One and one equals another one. Pleasure in the female is not a requirement. Pair-bonding is stronger in geese. We're not talking about love, we're talking about biology. That's how we all got here, daughter.

Snails do it differently. They're hermaphrodites, and work in threes.

7

Each Female Body contains a female brain. Handy. Makes things work. Stick pins in it and you get amazing results. Old popular songs. Short circuits. Bad dreams.

Anyway: each of these brains has two halves. They're joined together by a thick cord; neural pathways flow from one to the other, sparkles of electric information washing to and fro. Like light on waves. Like a conversation. How does a woman know? She listens. She listens in.

20 The male brain, now, that's a different matter. Only a thin connec- 20 tion. Space over here, time over there, music and arithmetic in their own sealed compartments. The right brain doesn't know what the left brain is doing. Good for aiming through, for hitting the target when you pull the trigger. What's the target? Who's the target? Who cares? What matters is hitting it. That's the male brain for you. Objective.

This is why men are so sad, why they feel so cut off, why they think of themselves as orphans cast adrift, footloose and stringless in the deep void. What void? she asks. What are you talking about? The void of the universe, he says, and she says Oh and looks out the window and tries to get a handle on it, but it's no use, there's too much going on, too many rustlings in the leaves, too many voices, so she says, Would you like a cheese sandwich, a piece of cake, a cup of tea? And he grinds his teeth because she doesn't understand, and wanders off, not just alone but Alone, lost in the dark, lost in the skull, searching for the other half, the twin who could complete him.

Then it comes to him: he's lost the Female Body! Look, it shines in the gloom, far ahead, a vision of wholeness, ripeness, like a giant melon, like an apple, like a metaphor for "breast" in a bad sex novel; it shines like a balloon, like a foggy noon, a watery moon, shimmering in its egg of light.

Catch it. Put it in a pumpkin, in a high tower, in a compound, in a chamber, in a house, in a room. Quick, stick a leash on it, a lock, a chain, some pain, settle it down, so it can never get away from you again.